CW00631203

SACRED QUEST

ROSS CLIFFORD and PHILIP JOHNSON

SACRED QUEST

A HARD LOOK AT TODAY'S SEARCH FOR WHOLENESS, MEANING AND PERSONAL TRANSFORMATION

AN ALBATROSS BOOK

© Ross Clifford and Philip Johnson 1993

Published in Australia and New Zealand by
Albatross Books Pty Ltd
PO Box 320, Sutherland
NSW 2232, Australia
and in the United States of America by
Albatross Books
PO Box 131, Claremont
CA 91711, USA

First edition 1993, published as
Shooting for the Stars
Second edition 1995, as *Sacred Quest*

*This book is copyright. Apart from any fair
dealing for the purposes of private study,
research, criticism or review as permitted
under the Copyright Act, no part of this book
may be reproduced by any process without
the written permission of the publisher.*

National Library of Australia
Cataloguing-in-Publication data

Clifford, Ross
Sacred Quest

ISBN 0 7324 1024 X

1. New Age movement. 2. Christianity and other religions.
3. New Age movement – Relations – Christianity.
I. Johnson, Philip, 1960– . II. Title.

299.93

Cover illustration: Michael Mucci
Printed and bound by Griffin Paperbacks, Netley, SA

Contents

FOR:
Keith and Marjorie, Beverley, Briony and Joel:
for their never-ending support.

FOR:
Justin Martyr
who showed us the path:
*'Reason directs those who are truly pious
and philosophical to honour and love
only what is true, declining to
follow traditional opinions
if these be worthless.'*
(AD 155)

Introduction

We value today's search for personal transformation. So we could not resist the opportunity of
checking out a major New Age festival in our
home town. Although the expression 'New Age'
is very popular, many seekers prefer labels
like 'New Sense', 'Age of Aquarius' or 'New
Consciousness'. We found this public exhibition
for spiritual pathways was touching many people
at key points in their quest for meaning and healing. We were so impressed by it that we wanted
to be active participants next time around.

To this end we rang the administrator's office.
There was real excitement over our proposal of
running a stall that featured healing through the
laying on of hands, prayer and a video on Jesus.
However, as the proposal began to unfold, clouds
of concern enveloped the conversation. 'Hey,
who are you guys? What's this all about?' We
then shared that we represented a group who

empathised with those who, like us, are involved in a spiritual pilgrimage. We wanted to share our journey with Jesus. Their hesitation was now most apparent. 'Let us think about this and call you back.' And they did!

It's not every day that one receives a call from Australia's ABC television. 'We hear that you have booked a stall at the festival. We are fascinated to know what Christians have in common with New Age type beliefs. Can we film your preparation and activities, and interview you interacting with New Age celebrities and practitioners?'

As our handouts, books and display units were packed, the cameras rolled. At our booth there was little privacy as conversations were filmed and prayers became public property. This all added to the drama of being involved in one of the world's foremost spiritual festivals.

Walking amongst the stalls made us feel that we were in a first century bazaar. 'Do you want your palm read?' 'Past lives healed!' 'Future wealth guaranteed!' 'Run your life by the stars!' 'Let me take you to the Other Side!' 'The cards tell it all!' 'This crystal will energise!' 'Chant this mantra!' 'Love this Ascended Master!' 'Your healing is within!' 'Visions are a reality!' 'Travel with North American Indians' spiritual ancestors!' 'In your aura find your halo!' 'Meet the Cosmic Christ!' 'Let us touch you!' 'Become a neo-pagan!'

We discovered that we 'belonged' in this

metaphysical smorgasboard as people like us were sincerely searching for the answers to the ultimate transformation questions in life:

* *Where do I find release from my brokenness?*
* *How do I cope with my illness?*
* *Where do I find peace?*
* *Where is the heart of love and acceptance?*
* *What path should I choose?*
* *Am I all that there is?*
* *How do I fulfil my dreams and live to my potential?*

As the festival doors closed for another year we were not denied final hugs and embraces from the astrologers, healers and psychics. We even felt free to say 'God bless you!'

A week or so later at our debriefing we asked ourselves, 'What was our lasting impression of the festival?' We concluded it was the number of people who sought us out and posed such questions as: 'What do the Judeo-Christian Sacred Writings and the Master Jesus say about the spiritual paths and techniques found at the festival? Are there "stars" that offer personal recovery and fulfilment of dreams? What beneficial advice do the Sacred Scriptures give?'

In this book we want to answer the questions asked of us by positively exploring the ways of transformation. This book is dedicated to those who know that life is more than dogma, that a vital spiritual experience is enriching and that it is undergirded by integrity.

This is the visionary age of the New Human who settles for nothing less than the road to recovery.

1

Encountering near-death experiences and global consciousness

I was going towards a very bright light. And as I was travelling along I could see different coloured lights and then I got stopped, just stopped before I got to the light. And I felt this extreme presence of love, just absolute love. And I heard very clearly. . . I was being confronted by my Creator. . . I was told it wasn't my time to go on — that I had to come back. I had my life's work to do.[1]

The New Age has little to do with prophecy or the imaging of a new world, but everything to do with the imagination to see our world in new ways that can empower us towards compassionate, transformative actions and attitudes. If we remember this, then we can forget the New Age of channels, crystals and charisma and get on with discovering and co-creating

*a harmonious world that will nourish and empower
all of us on this planet and all our children who will
be the inheritors of our future.*[2]

*'In my Father's house are many rooms; if it were not
so, I would have told you. I am going there to prepare
a place for you.'*[3]

'AS WE LAY HANDS ON HELEN, we ask that she
might be released from her painful back complaint
that she might have strength in her spine and will
know peace in her personal journey.' After our
prayers, Helen thanked us and joined her friends.
Peter and Carol had been observing us and came
over for a chat.

Peter and Carol represent an increasing number
of people who are exploring the realm of life beyond
the grave. Their forte is research in near- death
experiences (NDEs) and the comfort such happen-
ings have brought to many. We found that we
could celebrate together that death is not itself the
end of our existence. We were all aware of the
prominence given to such encounters by 'Donahue'-
style television programs.

They shared with us how Dr Kübler-Ross, the
recognised world authority on death and dying,
was dramatically moved from doubt to faith with
respect to near death experiences.

Kübler-Ross was going to quit her position at
the University of Chicago where she was dealing
with terminal patients. As she was walking in the

hospital, she encountered a former patient who had been dead for eleven months. The patient spoke to her, walked with her, touched her hand and opened the door for her office. The patient asked, 'Can you hear me?' and pleaded with Kübler-Ross, 'Promise that you won't give up your work.' (Kübler-Ross says that this was the most important message she has ever received.)

After these words, she stood in her study still in doubt and then this entity wrote a note for the pastor involved in her case. The note stated 'at home, at peace'. Kübler-Ross abandoned scepticism and within a few weeks of this event she began to write her best-selling book, *On Death and Dying*. Peter and Carol referred us to an article in *Simply Living* magazine where this story is told.[4]

Another benefit of near-death experiences for Peter and Carol is the move into the new paradigm of global consciousness. From the radio documentary, 'And When I Die, Will I Be Dead?' comes a story from Australia.[5] This tells of a schoolboy suffering from multiple heart attacks who departed his body and entered the spirit world.

On meeting his dead relatives, he was taught about life after death. They indicated that there is no personal judgment at death and that all spiritual paths are valid approaches. In today's global village, Peter and Carol see the need for a spiritual faith that embraces all of the traditions.

We took time to identify with Peter and Carol the common elements of near-death experiences.

Raymond Moody in his book *Life After Life* suggests fifteen such elements and *The Aquarian Guide to the New Age* succinctly identifies these in this way:

> *Common denominators seem to be the sensation of passing through a tunnel, an out-of-body experience, a perception of light and meetings with spiritual or biblical figures and/or dead friends and relatives. Individuals tend to interpret the experience in the light of their own cultural background.*[6]

When people experience the 'light', they often report being embraced by an immeasurable breadth of love that they find is indescribable.

❖ Testimonies for near-death experiences

As we agreed with Peter and Carol, the case for near-death experiences (NDEs) is very strong. The stage is being reached where most people know of someone who has had one. As well as this, there is the thorough documentation in the writings of Raymond Moody, Robert Monroe, Elizabeth Kübler-Ross, Cherie Sutherland, Maurice Rawlings, Tal Brooke, John Weldon and Zola Levitt.

The subject has also attracted some serious scholarship as evidenced in Carol Zaleski's doctoral work, *Otherworld Journeys*. She states: 'In nearly all cultures, people have told stories of travel to another world, in which a hero, shaman, prophet, king or ordinary mortal passes through the gates of death and returns with a message for the living.'[7]

International actress Elizabeth Taylor has recently spoken of her own NDE. She had kept quiet because it sounded so 'weird':

Thirty years ago I was pronounced dead — I've read my own obituary. I had a terrible case of pneumonia and I stopped breathing for five minutes. And while I was dead, I went on and on through a long tunnel until finally I saw a light at the end of it. The light was wonderful and I wanted to go into it. But Mike Todd was standing at the end of the tunnel and he said: 'You have to go back. You can't come over yet. You have to fight to go back.' So I did. . . I was painfully conscious of everything. Sounds, colours, objects, people. . . And when I heard that thousands of people had gathered outside the hospital and were praying for me, I felt an overwhelming sea of love being channelled into me. In a way that was almost mystical, I felt I was being accepted into humanity.[8]

Margaret, who is an acquaintance of ours, has related how her encounter had a fresh angle:

While in the tunnel I had a strange feeling as though something (my soul, I imagine) was being vacuumed out of my body (as if my body were a shell). Not painful, just strange. I remember vividly hearing someone (I presume to be God) saying to me, 'Are you ready to die?' My response was 'What about Deryck', to which I heard, 'He'll manage.' My next thought was 'It'll be a large funeral' and so I said, 'Yes, I am prepared to die.'

She found this to be an invigorating experience for her journey with Jesus.

Even the atheist philosopher Sir Alfred Ayer had an NDE during a bout of pneumonia. It didn't change his convictions about God, but surprisingly brought this response:

> *My recent experiences have slightly weakened my conviction that my genuine death, which is due fairly soon, will be the end of me, though I continue to hope that it will be.*[9]

Philosophers Gary Habermas and J.P. Moreland have established that NDEs are happening at all phases of medical demise. There are verified accounts of people having out-of-body experiences when they are close to being pronounced clinically dead. Then there are the ones when the heart stops and even after the brain stops. They conclude: 'Since human consciousness does not depend on the central nervous system (or other bodily activity), NDEs are evidence of at least a short period of life after death.'[10]

❖ Earth-plane explanations for NDEs

As one can imagine, the critics have pointed out a number of natural explanations for this phenomenon. These include:

* The possibility of time-travel where one moves out of linear time into another dimension of

consciousness where past, present and future are one. In this tunnel, one may be linking up with 'past' comrades. A creative story entitled *Many Dimensions* by novelist Charles Williams has explored some of these possibilities concerning time and consciousness.

* Carl Sagan, in *Broca's Brain,* suggests NDEs are a shadow recall of bliss in the womb. They are a reminder of our passage through the birth canal.

* A cardiac surgeon has told us that when someone is under the effects of anaesthetics, oxygen deprivation or high fevers, strange things can happen. It is therefore not wise to give any real weight to their post-operative recollections. Similar sensations can be experienced through hallucinogenic drugs. It should be noted, though, that various tests have established that the substantial majority of those who had an NDE were not affected by anaesthetics, lack of oxygen or drugs. As well, in many cases, there is no evidence of unusually high body temperature and one is not dealing with feverish delirium.[11]

* Some doctors note that when parts of the brain are shut down, one does lose one's bearings and a sense of drifting is common.

* Dr Zaleski, after making a major cross-cultural study, states that other world journey stories are 'through and through a work of the socially conditioned religious imagination'. She further comments that we can no longer insist that such visionary experiences paint 'a true picture of

what occurs at the extreme border of life'.[12] She affirms the positive benefit of NDEs, but is saying they are symbols that reflect our religious heritage rather than actual events.

* By this it is implied that, if you lived in Medieval Europe and had an NDE, you might see demons, hell-fire, saints and madonnas. If you were living in India, you would most likely encounter Krishna, Ram, Ganesh and so on. Consistent with Zaleski's insights are those of Zambian physician, Dr Nsama Mumbwe, who found that amongst Africans many interpreted their NDEs as evil. Half thought the experience signified that they were somehow 'bewitched'. Another called it a 'bad omen'.[13]

* NDE traveller and researcher Professor John Wren-Lewis states: 'A healthy discipline of scepticism is essential in evaluating NDE reports and it's equally important when looking for patterns in the data that might provide clues to what these experiences are really all about.'[14]

He then gives a possible explanation for the phenomenon in terms of an 'eternity consciousness'. He interprets our modern busy lifestyle as acting as a 'block' to confronting the existential reality of our own death. Instead, in the here and now we are solely concerned with survival. When people undergo an NDE, they may be simply coming in touch with a suppressed inner sense of eternity.

Of all these natural explanations, NDE expert Cherie Sutherland rightly says: 'Overall they tend to be more evaluative than descriptive, and so far they can only be considered speculative at best.'[15] We agree that science has not satisfactorily accounted for these metaphysical travels. As Melvin Morse asserts: 'The near-death experience remains a mystery.'[16] Whilst this is true, our awareness of the mystery of NDEs should be balanced by the excellent earth-plane research work of those like Dr Zaleski.

❖ The messages from the 'other side'

What we have noticed is there are profound spiritual messages coming from those who have been beyond the grave and back. In this spirit world, many are stressing harmony and unity. It does not appear to matter too much what path you choose, so long as you are earnest in your quest to experience the truth. The affirmation of these messages is recorded in Cherie Sutherland's book.

Peter and Carol sought to enhance this outlook by pointing us to the teaching of leading New Age, NDE and out-of-body experiences (OBE) researcher, Robert Monroe. He believes that our common earthly experiences positively equip us all for the other side:

This earth-life system is a predator world, so we can't help but be predators in order to exist in this world. We have come to this system for a very particular purpose, to learn certain things, and this system is exquisitely, beautifully adjusted to allow us to learn those things. We learn survival at a physical level and we learn to manipulate energy. We also learn cause and effect, authority and responsibility — all those things we learn here as humans. But I can assure you that, once you graduate from this earth-life system and move into other realities, you are God. You are God in those other realities because of what you have gathered here.[17]

Whilst we understood Peter and Carol's ideas, we wondered about those who have had NDEs and have found them not to be a good experience or a pointer to universal salvation. It is surprising that some current NDE researchers, unlike Dr Zaleski and *Psychology Today*, do not document some of these well-known cases. Perhaps this is because of their own New Sense bias.[17] In fact many, after NDEs, have been driven back to the conviction that there can only be one true path to take and that is found in Christ.

Dr Maurice Rawlings is a physician who has gathered together accounts of 'negative' NDEs, which actually drove him from scepticism to faith. He now even holds that some NDE encounters may be dark-spirit directed. In his first book, *Beyond Death's Door*, Rawlings recounts:

I was resuscitating a terrified patient who told me he was actually in hell. He begged me to get him out of hell and not to let him die. When I fully realised how genuinely and extremely frightened he was, I too became frightened. . . Now I feel assured that there is life after death and not all of it is good.[18]

The discovery of 'negative' NDEs in modern times has been confirmed by Dr Karlis Osis who records the terrifying experience of a patient who cried out, 'Hell, hell, all I see is hell.' Then there was the patient who had the sensation of being burned alive.[19] We recently were at a gathering where New Zealand scuba-diver Iain McCormack shared about being stung by the poisonous box jellyfish. He described his initial post-death experience as chilling and dark.

US psychiatrist George Ritchie had an extensive NDE where he saw people in a frightening and hellish place. It is interesting to note that NDE researcher Raymond Moody has written the foreword to Ritchie's book *Return From Tomorrow* and describes it as 'startling' and among one of the 'three or four most fantastic and well-documented' cases known to him.[20] Moody is best known for recounting positive NDEs.

In interviewing patients, Dr Rawlings has observed that there is a methodological problem with prominent NDE investigators like Moody and Kübler-Ross:

It then occurred to me that Dr Kübler-Ross, Dr Moody and other psychiatrists and psychologists were interviewing patients who had been resuscitated by other doctors several days to several weeks previously. Neither Kübler-Ross nor Moody, so far as I know, has ever resuscitated a patient or had the opportunity of recording immediate on-the-scene interviews.

After many interrogations of patients I have personally resuscitated, I was amazed by the discovery that many have bad experiences. If patients could be immediately interviewed, I believe researchers would find bad experiences to be as frequent as good ones. However, most doctors, not wanting to be identified with spiritual beliefs, are afraid to question patients about their after-death experiences.[21]

Cherie Sutherland, however, seems reluctant to accept the evidence of negative cases provided by Rawlings. In her second book, *Within the Light*, she dismisses his work in these terms:

Of negative reports that have surfaced in contemporary times, Maurice Rawlings' work is perhaps the best known, taking as it does an extreme view. In 1978, Rawlings presented the thesis that hellish NDEs are simply repressed. Arguing as he does, however, from a 'born-again' Christian perspective with the clear agenda of proving to readers the existence of hell and therefore the need to be 'saved', his presentation is questionable.[22]

A couple of points need to be noted concerning her criticisms of Rawlings' work. First, what she fails to report is that Rawlings was converted to faith from scepticism about life after death after he had resuscitated a patient who had a negative NDE. Rawlings then went on to research for other possible cases of negative NDEs. Next, Rawlings' findings have found support in research conducted by the famous US pollster George Gallup Jr in his 1983 book *Adventures in Immortality*.[23]

Tom Harpur is another NDE researcher who expresses some reservations about Rawlings' first book. However, Harpur is willing to make this concession: 'Rawlings at least has raised the issue that possibly all is not light and bliss during the near-death experience.'[24]

Rawlings has further documented even more negative NDEs in his recent book *To Hell and Back*.[25]

Finally, Margot Grey is a humanistic psychologist who has no religious ties whatsoever. In her book *Return from Death*, Grey documents several cases of negative NDEs where people experienced feelings of fear and panic. She reports that negative NDEs involve a black void, a sense of an evil force and encounters with a hell-like environment. As Grey holds no religious beliefs, her documentation can scarcely be criticised as being motivated by an agenda to convince her readers of the existence of hell.[26]

We shared with Peter and Carol, then, that not all the messages from the other side uphold global consciousness.

❖ Lazarus unveils the other side

Indirectly the Sacred Writings touch on these kinds of life after death experiences. There are the records of Paul's vision of the third heaven, Lazarus the brother of Mary and Martha being raised from the dead, and Jesus' teaching about the rich man and Lazarus. Although these passages are sometimes referred to by NDE exponents, it is interesting to note that none of them explicitly deals with the concept. Here all the characters involved in the experience affirmed their need of Christ. There is no indication that they had a sense that all is well in the after life. In fact, Paul went on to explicitly teach otherwise.

We suggested to Peter and Carol that, rather than entering into dogma, we should let the narrative of the poor man Lazarus speak to our hearts. We paraphrased it this way:

> *There was a baby-boomer who enjoyed the best things in life, but showed no compassion for the poor beggar Lazarus (perhaps because this was Lazarus' 'script' in life). Both the baby-boomer and Lazarus died. The baby-boomer found his destiny had brought him into a place of great alienation and torment, whereas Lazarus entered into a peaceful and wholesome rest.*
>
> *The baby-boomer recognised the folly of his life and begged to be rescued. He pleaded that his soul-mates might be warned as to what lies beyond the grave. He was told that the Sacred Scriptures are already there to enlighten them. Lazarus, on*

the other hand, in his peaceful rest communed with the great sage Abraham.[27]

❖ Insight

Near-death experiences are helping a growing number of people to cope with the trauma of death. They awaken us to the reality of eternity. Researchers and New Agers differ as to their meaning. Perhaps this is because the NDE traveller is still only on the fringe of the city glimpsing the city lights and is yet to fully explore down-town. The first impressions are therefore limiting and subjective.

Is there anyone who can guide us through this labyrinth? Is there anyone who has been down-town and back?

2

Understanding past-life therapy

> *That Origen (the early church leader) taught the pre-existence of the soul in past world orders of this earth and its reincarnation in future worlds is beyond question.*[1]

KESHA IS A PAKISTANI MYSTIC who is convinced that he has lived before. He said he is destined to live many more times. Kesha believes that the Sacred Writings contain examples of reincarnation and that the early church has suppressed this teaching. For him, the law of karma — what you sow you reap — is the best explanation for the existence of suffering and evil in the world.

He told us that reincarnation is important because, when we go into our past lives, we discover the karma that is catching up to us. This is therapeutic as it allows us to understand ourselves and perhaps to rescript our fate by positive, creative visualisation. Kesha himself explored his past lives by rebirthing. He went on to explain that our path of spiritual evolution is to progress through many lifetimes. Eventually we will reach a state of balanced karma and God-consciousness.

One of us connected with Kesha about the healing that comes from looking back. He mentioned that in his early teens, whilst for a short period living on the streets of one of our capital cities, he had suffered much abuse, hurt and rejection.

The pain this produced had caused him to suppress the memory. This had stopped him from dealing with questions of self-esteem and rejection that had come out of his teenage experience. It was only some twenty odd years later when visiting the city that in a divinely dramatic way the events were revived. And that resulted in an immediate understanding of why he lacked empowerment to assert himself in life. Regressing back revealed a hurtful past that he could now be healed of and released from.

We acknowledged with Kesha the healing that flows from looking back. Kesha then asked us whether our path, which certainly allowed for regression, did not also embrace reincarnation?

❖ John the Baptist's past life
Kesha suggested that reincarnation is found in Matthew 17, verses 10 to 13:

And the disciples asked Jesus, 'Why do the teachers of the law say Elijah must come first?' Jesus replied, 'To be sure, Elijah comes and will restore all things. But I tell you, Elijah has already come and they did not recognise him, but they have done to him everything they wished. In the same way, the Son of Man is going to suffer at their hands. Then the disciples understood that he was talking to them about John the Baptist.

In ancient Israel, there was an expectation that the prophet Elijah would return again as a herald of great deeds. He would bring healing to his people:

See, I will send you the prophet Elijah before that great and dreadful day of the Lord comes.[2]

This is a developing theme in the New Testament where the people were looking for his return. When Jesus spoke about John the Baptist, he said:

And if you are willing to accept it, he is the Elijah who was to come.[3]

The American trance medium, Edgar Cayce, poses this question about these passages:

What logical thought-process induced the disciples to draw such a conclusion so promptly, unless Jesus had made them thoroughly familiar with the laws of reincarnation?[4]

We pointed out to Kesha that there are hurdles with the above passages. The texts do not support the reincarnation of Elijah in the person of John the Baptist:

* As Elijah lived a truly enlightened life he by-passed death and was taken directly to heaven.[5] Such a sage has surely moved beyond the wheel of reincarnation.
* In the Matthew 17 passage, the story is also told of how Jesus appears on a mountain with the 'spirits' of Moses and Elijah. John the Baptist was already dead at this time. In reincarnation, the latest incarnation is the next stage. If the Baptist was truly Elijah reincarnated, then that incarnation would have appeared.
* John the Baptist himself specifically denied that he was literally Elijah:

    They asked him, 'Then who are you? Are you Elijah?' He said, 'I am not.'[6]

* The Sacred Scriptures clarify what these passages are all about. They reveal that John came 'in the spirit and power of Elijah'.[7] In other words, when Jesus was talking about John and Elijah he was not speaking about reincarnation, but the similarities in their ministries.

Another Sacred Writings passage may appear to lend support to reincarnation. Jesus told Nicodemus that 'no-one can see the kingdom of

God unless he is born again'. Nicodemus was puzzled by this and thought that he had to re-enter the womb. Jesus made it plain that this was not so. He said:

> I tell you the truth, no-one can enter the kingdom of God unless he is born of water and the Spirit. Flesh gives birth to flesh, but the Spirit gives birth to spirit.

Here Jesus does not refer to any cycle of reincarnation, but is indicating that to belong to God's kingdom you must be embraced by the Spirit of God. In fact, the meaning of the Greek word is more correctly translated as 'born from above' than 'born again'.[8]

❖ An integrating experience

As we talked, Kesha could see that for us the greatest stumbling-block with reincarnation is its incompatibility with resurrection. A careful comparison of various New Testament passages shows that Jesus and his disciples believed in the resurrection of the body from the dead.[9]

There is a real difference between reincarnation and resurrection. First, resurrection implies you die once.[10] Second, resurrection assumes that our eternal destiny is not lived separate from some bodily experience. In Judaism and Christianity, because the body is created by God it is good. Eastern religion and New Age thought is more along the lines of the Greek philosophy that the body is rudimentary and needs to be escaped. Princess Diana's astrologer, Penny Thornton, expresses this simply:

> *The planets seem to be pointing to an era when we transcend the lower 'animal' passions.*[11]

The resurrected body in the Sacred Writings is certainly a transformation of what we now know, but it can never be reduced to an 'out-of-body' destiny. As the Sacred Scriptures promise:

> *But our citizenship is in heaven. And we eagerly await a Saviour from there, the Lord Jesus Christ, who, by the power that enables him to bring everything under his control, will transform our lowly bodies so that they will be like his glorious body.*[12]

Significantly, the concept of the resurrection alters our life in the here and now. For example, as the body is indispensable it means that we must help the starving and the oppressed in practical ways. Surely this is seen in the devotion of saints like Mother Teresa. The resurrection also endows our inner psyche with the hope that our whole personality will live forever. Reincarnation, in contrast, only offers that our soul — after numerous journeys — will find a home in depersonalised consciousness.

❖ A tampering church
Kesha refocussed our thoughts by returning to a

commonly expressed concern about the Council of Constantinople (AD 553). The Council, he felt, censored the enlightened teaching of the early church father, Origen. And they scandalously heightened their sin by tampering with the reincarnation narratives in the Bible.

We suggested our first port of call be what Origen really said. A number of facts can be set out:

* In his earliest writings, Origen expressed a belief in the pre-existence of the soul.[13] By 'pre-existence', he meant that the soul was created before our earthly conception.
* Origen's belief in the pre-existence of the soul was only a personal speculation of his and not an official teaching held by the church. As a matter of principle, the pre-existence of the soul has nothing to do with whether we are reincarnated.
* Origen specifically denied the concept of the transmigration (reincarnation) of the soul after it had taken flesh. When speaking on the relationship between Elijah and John the Baptist, he exhorted:

> *In this place, it does not appear to me that by Elijah the soul is spoken of, lest I should fall into the dogma of transmigration (reincarnation), which is foreign to the church of God and not handed down by the apostles, nor anywhere set forth in the scriptures.*[14]

* At the Council of Constantinople, the only thing condemned was Origen's belief in the pre-existence of the soul. The Council did not even discuss reincarnation and there were no changes made to or tampering with the Bible.

We noted that it is evident from the above that the early church did not support reincarnation. In fact, the first mention made of it is by Justin Martyr who was born in about AD 114. Before he adopted Christianity, Justin studied in the schools of the Greek philosophers 'searching after some knowledge which would satisfy the cravings of his soul'.

Justin held that souls do not 'transmigrate into other bodies'.[15] Other prominent church leaders who rejected reincarnation and lived before this 'infamous' Council of Constantinople include: Irenaeus (c.175–195), Tertullian (c.160–220), Lactantius (c.260–330), Jerome (c.345–419), Gregory of Nyssa (c.335–395) and Augustine (354–430).

❖ Out-of-space reincarnation

Some modern theologians have proposed new ideas about life after death.[16] Their efforts are based on the desire to integrate the Western idea of resurrection with the Eastern idea of the immortality of the soul as expressed in reincarnation. The end product is that our bodies after death are replicated in another dimension or galaxy where the soul is linked with the new body (resurrection). This process seemingly is repeated through various 'beyond earth' pilgrimages until we attain *nirvana*, or cosmic oneness.

On the one hand, we have here a noble attempt to bring together the East and West. On the other hand, there is an attempt to explain how the resurrection of the dead can take place in a real way. As well as this, they are holding to the teaching of the Sacred Writings that we only die once on this earth plane.

A major problem for this unifying position is that neither the Christian Sacred Writings nor the Eastern Sacred Writings acknowledge such a merger between reincarnation and resurrection. This view is not part of the received body of the traditional teachings of the Masters. Clearly it has logical inconsistencies — we have already seen that there is a difference between reincarnation and resurrection.

Finally, in response to what some modern thinkers say, there is the teaching and experience of the great Master Jesus. He taught and experienced one complete resurrection and did not refer to out-of-space reincarnation. And he is the one who has a verifiable experience of life after death.

❖ Reworking evil

Kesha raised an important issue about the reason why people suffer in this world. He believed that whatever we do in this life determines the conditions and quality of our next life. This explains why young children in Ethiopia are dying of starvation. They apparently had undeveloped souls in their previous lives so the law of karma was now catching up with them.

Our minds went to the apostle John and his report on the blind man. Some suggest that here is an example of the law of karma:

> *As Jesus went along, he saw a man blind from birth. His disciples asked him, 'Rabbi, who sinned, this man or his parents, that he was born blind?'*

Isn't suffering here equated with past lives and deeds? Jesus' answer says otherwise:

> *Neither this man nor his parents sinned, but this happened so that the work of God might be displayed in his life.*[17]

Elsewhere, the Sacred Writings acknowledge that karma *in this life* can affect our well-being. Paul's adage was, 'You reap whatever you sow.'[18] The Bible does give some other answers for suffering, one being the world's and our chosen alienation from God. Whenever we are divorced from God's will, things go wrong. Another factor is that, because of our fallenness, we maltreat each other. The history of the world bears testimony to this.

It must also be admitted that the Sacred Scriptures indicate that suffering in God's hands can sometimes be a cause for spiritual growth. As Paul declares:

And we know that in all things God works for the good of those who love him, who have been called according to his purpose.[19]

We have found that the above rational answers will not normally satisfy an aching heart. We are hearing that many who are feeling comforted in reincarnation are not finding it in past lives explanations, but in the hope it brings of a continuing existence.

Lord Hailsham, the former Lord Chancellor of England, and one who has known personal tragedy in his own journey, reveals a certain hope:

When, in the autumn of October 1969, I saw the ruined homes in Belfast, burned out by my own fellow-citizens and fellow-Protestants out of sheer hatred of the occupants, I was deeply moved with horror and rejection, and all the cruelty and suffering which has gone on there since has only intensified my feelings on the subject. I will not, if I can avoid it, read stories of violence, or attend films or plays, or look at programs which portray evil. This is not because I believe such portrayals damaging to the soul, although I think they are, but simply because they hurt me too much. How can a good God permit such dreadful things to happen, I ask myself helplessly. . .

The one thing which keeps me sane in such moods of black despair is the memory of Christ's passion, his shameful conviction, his cruel mishandling, his slow death, and the ultimate hopelessness of his cry of dereliction from the opening words of

*the twenty-second psalm, and the belief, which I
have as a Christian, that this was not simply the
despairing cry of a good man, shamefully abused,
but a matter of cosmic significance, a statement that
God the invisible, the Creator, the ground of all
being, without body parts or passions, enters into
human suffering with us, and somehow agonises
in all our private Gethsemanes.*

*I know, of course, that this must necessarily be
folly to the Greeks, who can visualise a God in
human form well enough, as did Euripides when
he visualised Dionysius in the Bacchae, but cannot
visualise a God in suffering.*[20]

❖ The law of karma

In our conversation with Kesha, we raised some
problems we saw with his view of suffering, the
initial one being that many enlightened New Agers
hold that karma is not transmitted from a past life.
A number of 'Mind Powers' devotees accept the
concept of karma, but only believe we live on the
earth once. These pilgrims claim that by the power
of our thoughts we script for ourselves either good
or bad karma in the present and this determines
our non-earthbound future. This issue we will discuss in our chapter on mind powers.

Then there is the question that, if his view of
karma is correct, why do we not have any conscious
memory of our past deeds so as to avoid repeating
them in this present state? Even a session of hypnotic regression (recalling past lives under hypnosis)
or a rebirthing course (technique for awakening

primal experiences of pain) will not reveal all or even most of one's alleged past misdeeds. Without this vital knowledge, we are powerless to progress along the New Age path of spiritual evolution.

Another problem is the absence of the need for compassion for the victims of this world. When asked about such infamies as the Nazi death camps, famine victims, refugees and the victims of Hiroshima, Kesha's reply was: 'You don't have to worry about them at all! It is their karma!' This is in stark contrast to the compassion of Jesus when he fed, healed and delivered those who were oppressed and suffering.

Finally, we felt the major problem with karma is that it requires one to pull oneself up 'by one's own bootstraps'. We can never really be certain about the life we've lived or of reaching the final goal of release from this cycle of birth, death and rebirth. It all rests on our own performance and an impersonal cosmic law. In contrast, the Sacred Writings affirm an 'alien' new birth, a deliverance from our misdeeds by the death of the Master on the cross. There is no need for another life.

❖ The testimony of the many

Kesha continued to plead for reincarnation on the basis that it was in tune with the teachings of the 'Enlightened'. It is indisputable that many teachers in Hindu, Buddhist, Jain and Taoist traditions, as well as the ancient Greeks, have believed in some version of reincarnation.

Nonetheless, many other teachers such as Moses, Isaiah, Jesus, Muhammad and Viking sages have not accepted it. In this case, we suggested the spiritual path cannot be resolved by counting numbers; the truth lies elsewhere. Sad to say, eighteen million Australians, sixty million Britons — or a billion Chinese — can all be wrong!

❖ Plausible evidence of past lives

Kesha offered various types of evidence to prove we have lived before. One of these is the common experience we have had of *deja vu* — entering a place that appears familiar, even though you have never been there before. Some simply cite their own 'memory' of a past life. Another proof is past life recall under hypnotic regression.

Then there is the revealing of a past life through contact with the spirits of the dead. This same proof often comes with those who claim to have had contact with extra-terrestrial beings. Finally, there is the explanation that there is not enough time to complete one's 'mission' in a single life.

There is a basic physiological explanation for *deja vu*. It is the rapid assimilation of information by the senses before it is fully processed in the brain. Therefore reaction can precede the mind's processing of data. We are learning just how remarkable our minds are and how often the answer lies within us, not in some paranormal explanation.

On top of all this, it is possible to identify many

of the sources which act as a catalyst for these experiences. Could it not be a picture previously observed
but forgotten, or a prior visit to a similar place?

There are a number of feasible explanations of a
memory 'flash' that appear to take us to another life.
One is *deja vu*. Another is the gift of psychic
powers, like that of Dutch crime-solver Peter
Hurkos. Then there is the idea that we have been
influenced by a foreign spirit.

Ian Stevenson is a prominent reincarnation ad-
vocate and researcher. He admits the foreign spirit
theory must be taken seriously even though he
prefers the reincarnation hypothesis. In support of
the foreign spirit view is the corroboration Stevenson has compiled. He has cases of people having
memory flashes of living a life of someone who is
not yet dead.[21] The memory flash raises more questions than it answers.

The most interesting argument for reincarnation
is hypnotic recall. Some of the more spectacular
cases involve people speaking in ancient or foreign
languages and recalling historical events. One must
not be dismissive of such remarkable phenomena
unless the evidence demands otherwise.

Psychologists writing on these phenomena have
instructed us about the reliability of recall. One
typical report asserts:

> *Although hypnosis increases recall, it also increases*
> *errors. In their study, hypnotised subjects correctly*
> *recalled twice as many items as did unhypnotised*

*members of a control group, but also made three times
as many mistakes. During hypnosis, you are creating
memories.*[22]

A further point concerns the reliance on the
recent phenomenon of 'repressed memory
syndrome' as evidence of reincarnation. A number
of experts, such as Elizabeth Loftus and Richard
Ofshe, have underscored several limitations with
human memories. And within the courts, where
repressed memories are being cited in child sex
abuse cases, corroborating evidence is now regarded
as indispensable. (This is not to deny the suppression of memories, but highlights the fact that
repressed memories must be supported by some
external evidence.) Thus, to base one's belief in
reincarnation solely on repressed memories is not at
all satisfactory evidence.[23]

Apart from the evidence of psychology and the
Sacred Scriptures, there is the confessed pragmatism
of some New Age leaders. Dick Sutphen has admitted about recall: 'If there's a positive result, I
don't care what it is because it's served the individual well.' This raises the serious question, 'If it
appears to work, does this make it real?'

Another difficulty with recall concerns the fact
that there is at present more than one claimant to
the past life of Cleopatra. Many claim to have been
in a stable two thousand years ago! This evidence
leaves one with the question whether past lives are
not a creative wish fulfilment.

What must also be taken into consideration is the documented claims of such celebrated cases as Bridey Murphy. In the 1950s, great excitement was associated with the case of American housewife, Virginia Tighe, who recalled under hypnosis a previous life as Bridey Murphy in nineteenth century Ireland. She went into great detail as to place names and even spoke in an Irish accent.

Numerous critics have pointed out that, as a young child, Virginia Tighe spent much time with an Irish nanny who taught her 'other language' Gaelic and told her stories about old Ireland. It is therefore risky to base any case on such stories. Australian occult authority, Nevill Drury, states, 'The case remains controversial.'[24]

What of the claim that reincarnation is confirmed through the advice received from extra-terrestrials and spirit beings? There is one salient obstacle. These reports are unsubstantiated, even to the satisfaction of many New Agers.

The final argument for reincarnation is the need to have more time than life gives to fulfil our goals and so give meaning and purpose to our existence. We are all moved by the tragic loss of unfulfilled and seemingly incomplete lives. The trouble is that fulfilment could equally take place in another dimension — that being face to face with God. Why limit it to the earthly plane? Followers of the Master find comfort in the fact that their unfulfilled loved ones are maturing in the resurrected life found in the loving energy of Christ.

We were at a gathering where an African leader touched the audience as he opened up about the death of his young son. He found strength in the vision that his son is like a bud who will now blossom before the very heart of God. He intimated that they would be reunited and he would have the joy of discovering his son as a perfected personality.

❖ Group encounters and psychic unity

After our discussion about individual reincarnation, we drew Kesha's attention to group past-lives encounters. There are a number of cases coming to the fore. It appears that under hypnotic regression, members of a community recall past times together and mention similar data.

We recapped our previous concerns about the reliability of hypnotic regression. We mentioned one major case where both the facilitator and those involved did not accept that the experience was of a past life. Rather, they thought it was an expression of untapped psychic unity that has them playing out similar dreams to one another's. This suggests we want stories to live by — a theme which we explore in another chapter.

❖ Life through a rear-vision mirror

As our tête-à-tête with Kesha came to a close, we urged him not to be like those who are so overwhelmed by hurts that they limit themselves to the cleansing of past memories. Such can be a mediocre and contorted journey.

Popular writers Stan Katz and Aimee Kiu put it delightfully: 'It's a bit like trying to drive a car while looking only in the rear view mirror. You don't get very far that way and you run the risk of a crack-up. I prefer to check the rear view from time to time, making sure that the reflection is accurate, but concentrating most of my attention on the road ahead.'[25]

We have found strength in Jesus' exhortation to live an empowered life by putting our hand to the plough and not looking back. Paul the apostle is of the same mind: 'forgetting what is behind and straining towards what is ahead'.[26]

❖ Insight

Kesha in a most open way shared with us his deep feelings about reincarnation. Reincarnation affirms the belief we hold in common with Kesha: that there is life after death and that existence is more than material. The illuminating call of today is for people to rediscover eternity. We shared our view that he was mistaken about his belief that reincarnation was in the Sacred Writings and that it had been taught by Jesus and his early followers.

As we shook hands, there was the embracing warmth experienced by those who know what it is to yearn for healing. We offered Kesha an eternal healing of mind, body and spirit. This is found in the One who has transcended all our karma and the burden of the cycle of the wheel of life.

3

Learning from the Magi astrologers

The first place must beyond dispute be accorded to astrology, the most ancient and noble (divination) of them all. . . Astrology gained such credit among men of all peoples of the world that it was the only branch of occult science which the church dared not formally condemn.[1]

Astrology is basically about self-awareness. . . It's about who you are and why you are here.[2]

MATT WAS AN ASTROLOGER who we knew was a colossus amongst his peers. He proved to be one of the most interesting people we met at the festival.

Matt remarked: 'It's great to see you Christians here. So often I find Christians very hostile to the sorts of pathways being explored at this festival. My own pathway to personal recovery and global harmony is astrology.' We asked Matt: 'What kind of astrology do you use?' He responded that his interest was 'judicial astrology' — the conviction that the stars at the time of birth set forth your personality traits and the direction of your life.

We reached for the local newspaper and read one of our horoscopes. The starguide had forecast this person was going to enter into strong new relationships. 'Is this the kind of astrology you're into?'

Matt laughed. 'No, it's a little bit more sophisticated than that. The pop stuff is not all that accurate — it's just for fun. Astrology to be precise must be calculated on the exact minute of your birth to discover what planet is ruling in the constellation you were born under. As well, the location of the sun and other planets at that time is vital.'

'Do you hold to the ancient concept of the zodiac?' we interjected.

'Yes,' Matt replied. 'Stretched across the night sky is a band called the zodiac. As you look at the focal point on the band you discover what constellation is in vogue and where the sun, stars and planets are in relationship to it. Each of the constellations has a sign like Aries and will appear at the focal point of the band some time during the twelve-month cycle. Other factors include the influence of comets and eclipses on a person's horoscope.'

We replied: 'Would you see "natural astrology" which deals with the influence of the planets on the tides and weather being incorporated into astronomy and meteorology?'

Matt responded: 'That stuff is for the news weatherman.'

Our new friend Matt then challenged us to assimilate into our path the benefits that judicial astrology brings. He had an unshakeable confidence in astrology as a guide to life. He looked to the stars as a means of helping himself and others recover from past hurts. This was for him the way to find strength to lead a more productive life in relationships, business and health.

Matt concluded: 'Do you realise that astrology is in the Sacred Writings — that Christians have constantly dabbled in it?'

We indicated that we were keen to explore his path for recovery with him.

❖ The Magi astrologers

We invited Matt to join us as we connected with the path taken by one of the most famous groups of ancient astrologers: the Magi. Long before the birth of Jesus, Babylon was the multi-cultural centre of the fertile crescent. It boasted many prophets, priests and sages who forecast the future.

In their midst flourished the Magi, a class of wise ones who devoted their lives to the study and interpretation of stars. They were noted for lining up the births of significant people with cosmic signs. British scholar Richard France reports:

Astrological interest in Babylon and other parts of the East is well attested. . . The belief that the birth of great men was heralded by special stars is also widely attested.[3]

We reminded Matt that Nebuchadnezzar was Babylon's most famous king and he customarily consulted the Magi. At a crucial point in his reign Nebuchadnezzar had a mysterious dream, but its interpretation eluded the wise ones. It was at this time that the Magi were joined by a spiritually gifted Jew named Daniel.

Daniel was a Jewish exile whose reputation for prophetic gifts and understanding of dreams was widely regarded. He counselled Nebuchadnezzar about the limitations of the stars for personal guidance:

No wise men, enchanters, magicians or diviners can show to the king the mystery that the king is asking, but there is a God in heaven who reveals mysteries, and he has disclosed to King Nebuchadnezzar what will happen at the end of days.[4]

As Daniel unfolded the truths the king sought, he was appointed the chief of the astrologers.[5]

❖ The star of Jacob

Under Daniel's influence, the Magi came into contact with the Jewish Sacred Writings. These books recorded ancient predictions about Israel. One of these, known as the Oracle of Balaam, forecast the coming of a spiritual master whose presence would be known by a heavenly sign:

The oracle of one whose eye sees clearly, the oracle of one who hears. . . and whose eyes are opened. . . A star will come out of Jacob; a sceptre will rise out of Israel.[6]

Matt was not familiar with this oracle. We explained it was a prophecy about a mighty one, a descendant of Jacob the tribal elder of Israel. This mighty one would arise in a far off time and his presence would be signified by a star. That Balaam's oracle was well-known and widely circulated in various, but corrupted forms is seen in the writings of the Roman historian Tacitus.[7]

Several centuries were to elapse before the Magi could positively identify 'Jacob's Star'. Many feel that the star was the 6 BC configuration between Jupiter (known in astrology as the King's planet), Saturn (the shield of Palestine) and Mars in the constellation of Pisces. The Wise Men travelled from Babylon to Jerusalem to find the Palestinian king whose birth was indicated by this sign.

The Magi were probably guided by more than just Balaam's oracle. As mentioned, Daniel predicted the future. He declared that the coming of the Messiah would occur before the destruction of the rebuilt temple in Jerusalem.[8] The Magi would have been aware of the political disquiet in Palestine at the time of Jesus' birth. History reveals that the Temple was destroyed by the Romans in AD 70.

So the intriguing picture is of the Magi astrologers looking to the stars to connect them with the One foreshadowed by Balaam and Daniel. Their wish came true. The Sacred Scriptures tell their story and, when they located the Christ-child, they worshipped him:

> *When they saw that the star had stopped, they were overwhelmed with joy. On entering the house, they saw the child with Mary his mother; and they knelt down and paid him homage. Then opening their treasure chests, they offered him gifts of gold, frankincense and myrrh.*[9]

❖ The Mazzaroth

Matt was taken with the story of the Magi. He believed that the Sacred Writings also support the use of the stars for casting horoscopes that bring personal guidance for our lives today. One commonly cited passage referred to by astrologers is found in the book of Genesis:

> *And God said, 'Let there be lights in the dome of the sky to separate the day from the night; and let them be for signs. . .'*[10]

The inference here is that the stars as signs have a spiritual message which can be decoded. Our friend Matt placed great weight on this saying that even the Bible has judicial astrology. Whilst we can appreciate this view, it is not supported by the text. The stars are only evidence here of there being a Creator of our universe and its structures. As King David sang: 'The heavens are telling the glory of God; and the firmament proclaims his handiwork.'[11]

Matt also claimed support from a lesser known passage in the book of Job, where it reads:

Can you bind the chains of the Pleiades, or loose the cords of Orion? Can you lead forth the mazzaroth in their season, or can you guide the Bear with its children? Do you know the ordinances of the heavens? Can you establish their rule on the earth?[12]

The term *mazzaroth* is an ancient word for the zodiac and the references to the constellations of Pleiades, Orion and the Bear are believed to reinforce the idea that judicial astrology is looked upon favourably here. The difficulty with this is that these words are only affirming that there is a zodiac (position of the stars) and constellations — concepts held by both the astrologer and astronomer. It is not a passage that speaks of casting horoscopes, but describes in a poetic way the intricacies of the observable heavens. It is a passage that both the believer in astrology and the sceptic could affirm.

In fact, the context of the verse warns Job not to lose his faith in God in the hard times as he is the one who controls all things.

Indeed, the Sacred Scriptures draw attention to

the dangers of pursuing personal guidance from the stars as opposed to positively connecting with the Creator. As we have recognised, Daniel, the chief of the Magi, spoke against relying on the stars in this way. Isaiah the sage declared:

> *Stand fast in your enchantments and your many sorceries, with which you have laboured from your youth; perhaps you may be able to succeed, perhaps you may inspire terror. You are wearied with your many consultations; let those who study the heavens stand up and save you, those who gaze at the stars, and at each new moon predict what shall befall you. See, they are like stubble, the fire consumes them; they cannot deliver themselves from the power of the flame.*[13]

❖ The popularity of astrology

At this juncture Matt raised with us the exploding popularity of judicial astrology. He told us that he was personally aware of a growing number of Christians who are enchanted with the stars. We indicated that this fascination was not supported by the early church which was the repository of the Master's and his disciples' teachings. An early respected witness to this is the second century treatise *The Teaching of the Twelve Apostles*, commonly known as *The Didache*. In its instruction on 'the way of life', it unfolds this principle:

> *Do not be a diviner, for that leads to idolatry. Do not be an enchanter or an astrologer or a magician.*

Moreover, have no wish to observe or heed such practices, for all this breeds idolatry.

This principle was difficult for Matt to accept since he had firmly based his own road to recovery on the zodiac. He reiterated to us the undeniable trend among many modern Christians to dabble in astrology in their search for meaning and self-discovery. We agreed with Matt that their drive for meaning and direction has sadly often not been addressed by the church. We decided to delve more deeply.

❖ 'Outing' Christian astrologers

Our probing brought us to the early Protestants of the sixteenth and seventeenth centuries, many of whom were both active astronomers and astrologers. This is a fact which most Christians are unaware of. As one historian of the occult, John Warwick Montgomery, reports:

Many theologians of the Reformation period, such as Melanchthon, engaged in astrological activity. Luther, however, was not strongly pulled in this direction; he remarked on one occasion that his friend Melanchthon pursued astrology 'as I take a drink of strong beer when I am troubled with grievous thoughts'.[14]

Two of the early Protestant fathers of modern astronomy, Tycho Brahe and Johann Kepler, were also vigorous astrologers who cast their own personal horoscopes and forecast weather patterns by natural astrology. Across the Channel, Oliver Cromwell consulted the famous English astrologer, William Lilly.

It is worth noting that on the whole these astronomer-astrologers were prominent supporters of Copernicus. It may be remembered that Copernicus was the one who found that the sun was at the centre of the solar system. And that discovery was in a real sense later confirmed by Kepler who formulated the laws of planetary motion.'

We paused to consider what motivated them. Our discovery was that they were drawn to the heavens because they resonated with the work of an 'eternal architectural mind'. Kepler aptly expressed that they were not into astrology for the sake of it, but it focussed their lives on the One beyond the stars. Kepler said:

> I thank thee, O Lord, our Creator, that thou hast permitted me to look at the beauty in thy work of creation; I exult in the works of thy hands.[15]

In fairness to these sixteenth and seventeenth century Christian leaders, it should be said they found their surest guide to existence in dependence on Jesus and the Sacred Writings. Even when they toyed with horoscopes, they were never trapped into accepting that the stars ruled and life was fatalistic.

Further, whilst they had some leanings towards judicial astrology, their primary labours were directed at developing the more precise science of astronomical and meteorological calculations concerning the motions of the planets, stars and comets. Their overall outlook is seen in their affirmation of the teaching of social critic Johann Valentin Andreae, a friend of Kepler:

> *It is an uncertain thing to make everything dependent on the first moment of existence and birth. . . The most fortunate horoscope is that of adoption into the ranks of sons of God, whose Father, when consulted by prayer, rarely is silent upon anything; when besought rarely refuses anything, so far is it from him to expose them to wanderings of the stars. The wanderer on the earth realises this; and in the shadow of God he fears no storms of the sky.[16]*

❖ Links between Christianity and the zodiac

A novel but lesser known attempt to integrate the zodiac with Christianity concerns the efforts of two nineteenth century writers, Joseph Seiss and Ethelbert Bullinger. These thinkers believed that the message of Jesus can be correlated with the signs of the zodiac. They believed that the stars were a cosmic witness to the coming of Christ.[17]

For example, 'Virgo the virgin' is maintained to be a foreshadowing of the birth of Christ. It is claimed that the name of one of the stars in this constellation means literally 'the seed'. Therefore, the two central characters of the Christmas story — maiden and child — are present and this predates the prophecy of Isaiah 7: 14:

The virgin will be with child and will give birth to a son, and will call him Immanuel (NIV).

Whilst this position is stimulating, it is also speculative. It does maintain that the role of the stars is to lead people to God in Christ. It even takes seriously nature's link with the human journey. Perhaps if humankind had not lost its link with Paradise, the stars would more clearly reveal God's blueprint for the world.

❖ Astrology as a science

Matt asserted that judicial astrology is indeed scientific. By this we assumed he meant two things. First, it is scientific due to the precise measurements of the star charts. Second, it is a scientific tool for revealing the genetic and psychological makeup of people.

(a) The question of the precise measurement of the stars

Astrology is based on the view that the earth is at the centre of the solar system. However, as we indicated before, we are now children of the Copernican revolution. This means that the astrologers are wrong in projecting their forecasts on the basis of the planets' interactions with a fixed earth. Also we know of the existence of more planets (Uranus, Neptune, Pluto) than the ancient astrologers were aware of. Surely these extra planets raise questions as to the precision of traditional astrology as a science.

Modern astrologers have tended to dismiss the

problem by saying that the new discoveries make their science more exact. And then there are the asteroids which we now know dominate the sky. What about their potential impact on our star-charts?

(b) The question of the genetic and psychological makeup of people

Astrologers claim that the position of the planets at the precise moment of your birth gives you a natal chart which shows you your genetic makeup. Matt illustrated this by saying that the stars hold the key to understanding crime. He indicated that the horoscopes of both the victim and the criminal contain their roles. There is no need for punishment here. Astrology can help you understand yourself and enable you to rewrite your script.

There is no disputing that we as people are subject to genetic influences. The influence of heart disease and such genetically influenced illnesses on a family's medical history is a documented fact. But to assert that this is correlated to the planets is at best conjecture.

Genetic scripting was explored by the French astronomer Paul Couderc who tested the oft-made claim that musical ability relates to the birth-time position of the sun. After looking at over 2 000 horoscopes of musicians, he concluded:

> *The position of the sun has absolutely no musical significance. The musicians are born throughout the*

*entire year on a chance basis. No sign of the zodiac
or fraction of a sign favours or does not favour them.
We conclude: the assets of scientific astrology are
equal to zero, as is the case with commercialised
astrology. This is perhaps unfortunate, but it is a
fact.*[18]

Matt was keen for us to consider the work of
Michel Gauquelin, a scientist at the University of
Paris, who has researched astrology for over thirty
years. He told us how Gauquelin tested the influence of Mars on 2 088 sports champions at the
time of their birth. The statistical results were significantly in favour of a correlation.

However, Matt was unaware that Gauquelin
was not himself convinced about astrology. He did
further detailed tests on astrologers where he asked
them to match up people's characteristics with their
horoscopes. The results were dismal. Leading
astrologer Richard Nolle has asserted that these later
findings of Gauquelin's have been ignored for many
years. Gauquelin concluded:

*It is now quite certain that the signs in the sky which
presided over our births have no power whatever to
decide our fates, to affect our hereditary characteristics
or play any part however humble in the totality of
effects, random and otherwise, which form the fabric
of our lives and mould our impulses to action.*[19]

As for one's psychological makeup, there are

surely more complex influences than the planets. Serious astrologer Mary Coleman sees dangers in 'boxing' people into 'types' simply on star signs.[20] Further, the Sacred Writings identify the cause of our deep psychological soul-sorrow as being our separation from the Eternal Creator and not as being determined by the stars. Augustine echoed this yearning: 'You have made us for yourself, O God, and our hearts are restless until they rest in you.'

The remedy for this inner longing is spiritual reconciliation.

❖ Astrology works!

Another common response to why we should be involved in judicial astrology, apart from biblical and scientific grounds, was that it works. Matt was a pragmatist in this regard. We can identify with this.

When we considered our astrological profiles in a well-known horoscope decoder, we found that for one of us the personality portrayed was 'spot on'. For the other, it must be admitted, it well and truly missed the mark. It has been our experience that, at times, astrology can appear to be correct, but at others it is completely wrong. We believe one reason for this is that in the areas of personal guidance astrology has biblical and scientific limitations. As well, a general psychological profile is likely to ring true in some cases. Former astrologer Charles Strohmer brings this sobering thought:

As much as a person can be, I was into astrology for almost eight years. And I stayed with it because it 'worked'. I thought that this was good enough reason to stick with something. In July 1976, I found out that this was not reason enough. This may seem obvious, but not until then did I grasp that just because something 'works', it is not necessarily synonymous with what is right and true. That a thing works does not mean that it should be used. Some things when they work explode and maim. . . Mars doesn't rule Aries; Venus doesn't rule Libra; Jupiter doesn't rule Sagittarius; Mercury doesn't rule Gemini. But God the Lord does have rule over all things. Pray to hear the impassioned plea that crackles in his voice.[21]

❖ Insight

Our exploration of astrology has shown that it is indeed in the Sacred Writings. When it is mentioned, though, the stress is not on personal guidance from the stars. Rather the scrolls ask why one should seek guidance from the 'rocks' of the universe when one can go to the source of the universe. The Magi discovered the true role of the stars in the Sacred Scriptures is to lead us to God in Christ. They found the path to transformation in him. This is precisely the same 'therapy' those Christian astrologers referred to above relied on.

As our conversation with Matt concluded, he suggested that one of us supply him with details of our exact time of birth so that he could do a horoscope. This was embarrassing since for personal reasons the one he asked did not have access to this information. Matt then could not help out with this 'scientific' tool in mapping out our destiny and suggesting a process for personal recovery. The sense of rejection experienced was intense. When it was pointed out to Matt that he could not touch the lives of many in need, he appeared to feel the pain. He had been a good friend.

In contrast to the evident limitations of Matt's astrology, there comes the universal and unlimited call of the Master:

Come to me, all of you who are tired from carrying heavy loads, and I will give you rest. Take my yoke and put it on you, and learn from me, because I am gentle and humble in spirit; and you will find rest.[22]

4

Knowing cosmic oneness

There is one God. There is one intellect, which is God's intellect. There is one body, which is God's body. You are a part of God.[1]

Please note that for me, the words Higher Self, Creative Source and God are interchangeable terms.[2]

Does it make any difference that I call it Christ and she calls it the Force? Energy is energy. To my mind, it is of greater importance that we recognise the light in each other — and this applies to anyone with whom I come into contact.[3]

'I and the Father are one.'[4]

SALLY IS OUR 'GROUP ENTITY'. She is a representative name for all those who shared with us most passionately about their 'oneness' with God and nature.

Sally said there is only one essence or reality and that is consciousness or energy. We discover this in our 'higher self'. How do we do this? 'We do so by using visualisation, meditation, mantra or other spiritual technologies.'

Sally knew her 'discovery' was by no means new. The concept of all being one is found in certain forms of the Hindu faith and other religious expressions. It is called monism. In New Age parlance, it is often illustrated by the analogy of the universe as a lake. The lake is made up of many different droplets of water, each being of the same substance.

This illustration highlights the tremendous respect for *diversity* of personhood in New Age thought, whilst preserving one essence. This is something which is not always found in classical Eastern monism, where personhood is an illusion — simply, all is one.

The bottom line of oneness is the god factor. As all is one essence, all is god (pantheism). Consequently, we are god. Sally shared with us that our oneness is not primarily personal, but a force. This force allows us to control our own lives and create our own destinies. There was a sense of power and confidence in Sally's words: 'It is what all the great masters and gurus have spoken of.' We have met lots of people who have been uplifted, transformed and motivated by the realisation of their own divinity.

Marianne Williamson encapsulates the dream:

*Just as a sunbeam can't separate itself from the sun
and a wave can't separate itself from the ocean, we
can't separate ourselves from one another. We are
all part of a vast sea of love, one indivisible divine
mind.*[5]

It would be fair to say that at the heart of the
New Age faith is the belief in oneness. It has an
impact in the areas of belief, practice, dreams, healing, business, education, politics, science and
religion. Sally confided that the only way to overcome all the heartache, hurts and poor self-esteem
in the world is to recognise our divinity within.

As Sally spoke, we could hear the melodic singing from those on the platform behind us that we
are angels — not in the sense that we were created
as such, but in a heavenly sense. The apparent
well-being it produced in the faces of the crowd
who joined in was a testimony to the depth of their
experience.

❖ The masters on oneness
One major issue which Sally raised was her strong
conviction that cosmic oneness — where everything
that is is of the same substance — is something that
all of the world's religious masters have taught.
So we talked about the teachings of prominent
spiritual leaders.

As we did, we saw that many of them did not
espouse oneness:

* *Moses*. He taught that God was personal and separate from creation. As the psalmist poetically portrayed: 'What are human beings that you are mindful of them, mortals that you care for them? You made them a little lower than God. . . O Lord, our Sovereign, how majestic is your name in all the earth!'[6]

* *Pharaoh Rameses*. As Pharaoh of Egypt, Rameses was a human manifestation of one of the Egyptian gods, Amon-Re. Of all the people in Egypt, Pharaoh alone was considered to be a god. The religion of ancient Egypt was polytheistic (many gods).

* *Krishna*. He was primarily a personal god, even though the Hindu concept of Brahman is ultimately pantheistic.

* *Zoroaster*. He believed that there is a good Supreme Being called Ahura Mazda and an equal entity of evil named Angra Mainyu: 'From the beginning of existence there have been two inherently incompatible, antagonistic spirits in the world.'[7]

* *Jesus*. He taught that God was a supreme and personal being, One with whom we can have a relationship. He saw that we were not gods in a divine sense, but rather his created children who were to worship him. The fact that there is evil in the world — that all is not one or of God — is seen in Jesus' rebuke of Satan: 'It is written, "Worship the Lord your God and serve him only".'[8] When Jesus stated that 'I and the Father are one', he was not speaking of a cosmic oneness that we can all share in, but rather of

his unique relationship with the Father.

* *Paul the apostle.* When a crowd desired to worship him and Barnabas as gods, he cried: 'We, too, are only men — human like you!'[9] Paul also believed in a supreme personal being.

* *Muhammad.* He taught that Allah alone was God and the only One worthy of worship. He commanded the execution of any person who presumed to accept the worship which was only rightfully belonging to Allah.

* *Leif Eriksson the Viking.* Like other Viking warriors, he believed in various gods such as Thor the god of Thunder. He looked forward to a place in Valhalla along with all other warriors after death.

* *'Abdu'l-Baha.* He was an early leader of the Baha'i faith and taught that the other enlightened teachers were only messengers sent by the one God. The Baha'i hold to a separate creator God.

❖ Christ and cosmic consciousness

Many visitors to our booth at the festival engaged in conversation with us over the meaning of the commonly used New Sense phrase, 'the Christ consciousness'.

One person suggested: 'It is just another way of explaining cosmic oneness.'

Another said: 'It's the idea that within each one of us there is a divine spark which allows us to see ourselves as part of God. Jesus the man became enlightened to this truth and acts as our model.'

Several took up the theme of the divine spark in Christ and proposed 'that this now self-realised Jesus awakens the Christ consciousness in us all. This rebirth can also be called a cosmic consciousness.'

From our inquirers, there was an oft-quoted passage from the sacred texts which they believed spoke of this divine spark within us all: 'The kingdom of God is within you.'[10]

The author of these words, Luke, who also wrote Acts, was not directing us to a divine light within, when he quoted these words of Jesus. As we have already noticed, this same author records the denial that Paul and Barnabas had any divinity/Christ consciousness. The question that remains is what the words of Christ mean. It would be true to say the words 'within you' can also be translated from the Greek as 'amongst you'. When the context of the whole passage is considered, it is hard to escape the conclusion that Jesus is merely teaching that, if you know him, you are a part of his kingdom.

Whilst Jesus' kingdom has an outward dimension that seeks to alleviate injustice, oppression and spiritual poverty, it would be crippling to miss that it has an inner personal realm. This internalised aspect of the kingdom, though, is not about our own divine consciousness. Rather what Luke records is the human being receiving the aid of the Holy Spirit for living the kingdom life.[11]

Another positive sharing with Sally about Christ consciousness concerned the very meaning of the word 'Christ'. In the Sacred Writings it means the 'Anointed One'. It is the Greek translation for the Hebrew word 'Messiah'. The Hebrews looked for just one future messiah and not a tribe of anointed/divine ones. To apply the concept of cosmic consciousness to the Sacred Scriptures is to give to them a meaning which is not even available if you read them in a mystical way.

Even more compelling is the fact that, in the Sacred Gospels, Jesus through his resurrection is revealed as the one who is more than human. When Thomas the doubter received enlightenment about this, he affirmed Jesus as his God and was not driven to any sense of his own divine consciousness. The Gospels conclude with a note of Jesus worship, not higher self: 'When they saw him, they worshipped him; but some doubted.'[12]

❖ We are the 'connected world'

In our discussions with Sally, we were again reminded that an important aspect of life is learning from each other. We had differences in our world views that would affect every aspect of our belief and practice — important differences as to whether we are God or as to whether the Creator is separate from his creation, questions that go to the heart of reality.

Nevertheless, in our being there was a sense of solidarity. The New Sense value of oneness has reminded us of our interconnectedness in a global village. As the poet John Donne so eloquently wrote: 'No man is an island unto himself.' And, as

Paul today would admonish the Church in Christ, there is 'neither Jew nor Greek, slave nor free, male nor female, for you are all one in Christ Jesus'.[13]

Australian New Sense writer, Richard Neville, sees our 'connectedness' like this:

> *We are all connected. And each of our actions or thoughts is linked to the global community and our own well-being. . . The choice of our morning drink, whether coffee or carrot juice, will have an impact on our metabolism, on the soil and probably on the economy of a distant land. Is the coffee we're drinking a cash crop, grown on an African plantation at the behest of the World Bank? Is it impoverishing the villagers by denying them land to cultivate their own gardens, or impoverishing the soil by draining it of nutrients, or impoverishing the economy by making it overly depend-ent on the vagaries of commodity prices?*[14]

❖ Peering through a distorted telescope

It should be acknowledged that real oneness is not just a human dimension, but involves the whole of nature. Sadly, some pilgrims need to be goaded to rediscover that we must not separate our concerns for justice and care for humans from care for the animals and land.

This separation had its roots in the French philosopher, Réné Descartes, who in the seventeenth century divided mind from matter. With Galileo's telescope we had the precedent where humans be-came mere observers of the natural world. We have dissected it bit by bit.

Together, we are striving to reverse this by joining with the beached whale and protecting the forest. Genesis 1 brings us this sense of sacred solidarity with all of nature by reminding us that we ourselves are created from dust. As scientist Paul Davies tells us, the very dirt we are made of comprises star-dust. Psalms 96, 98 and 148 declare that the trees, sun, seas, rivers, mountains, wind, stars and birds join in the dance of the praise of God. And Romans 8: 22 announces that the whole of creation groans for earth-healing.

❖ Gaia

A powerful motif for reconnecting us with each other and nature is Gaia (Greek goddess of the earth). Its classical myth-form is found in the ancient belief in an Earth-Mother. Gaia now has a meaning beyond this and calls us to see the whole world as a living, interconnected entity.

We affirm a global vision. It is time for the world to unite in a common agenda for eco-justice, peace, human dignity and freedom. Such a vision was expressed in a little-known stanza from Charles Wesley's eighteenth century hymn, 'Hark The Herald Angels Sing', which expresses joy at the global consequences of Jesus' coming:

> *Joyful, all ye nations rise,*
> *Join the triumph of the skies;*
> *Universal nature say:*

'Christ the Lord is born today.'
Now display thy saving power,
Ruined nature now restore,
Now in mystic union join
Thine to ours and ours to thine.[15]

❖ Another side of oneness

Tragically, a journey into the path of cosmic oneness can be like a trip into a dark tunnel which gets deeper and deeper with no exit from the lostness. It can be a black hole that 'sucks everything into itself'. Well-known writer on mysticism, Karen Armstrong, cautions:

> Entering the depths of the mind can be extremely dangerous if the would-be mystic has not the mental or physical capacity for this interior quest.[16]

Tal Brooke, a former disciple of Indian guru Sai Baba, speaks of his own chilling exposures:

> When a guru, a Rider, emerges from Explosion, you have his revelations, his claimed experiences and his non-human personality operating behind a poker face. Like a good screen actor, he can manipulate every button of human reaction, but behind it is a cold, unknowable, non-human intelligence. Who is the Rider? Who or what is occupying the body? [17]

❖ Quantum leap

Our time with Sally raised another significant issue with respect to oneness. Perhaps the most sophisticated expression of this concept today is found in the writings of the Austrian physicist, Fritjof Capra.[18] He holds that current developments in science — relativity theory, chaos theory, quantum theory — have led to new insights in physics. He finds parallels between atomic matter and aspects of Taoist and Buddhist faith. Capra maintains that, as energy and matter are now to be seen as one in process, the result is there is no real distinction between them. The same can be said for the scientist (object) and his experiment (subject): all is one.

An American physicist who has quested beyond purely material explanations of matter is Fred Alan Wolf. In *The Eagle's Quest*, he joins together the ecstatic visions of the tribal shaman into other worlds with that of quantum physics. True consciousness is that there are no personal boundaries; we are all part of the energised 'Big Dreamer'. We script the universe.

Understandably, some non-scientists are impressed by what Capra and Wolf have expounded. However, their views have not attained wide-spread acceptance amongst their peers. Scientists agree that the new insights in physics are now moving us out of the Newtonian-mechanical model of the world. Very few hold that it is leading us to monism. Even now, Capra admits there is room for classical Christianity in his new paradigm.[19]

Australian biologist, Charles Birch, suggests that it points to pan*en*theism (i.e. a natural God who develops in partnership with the world).[20]

Biochemist, Darryl Reanney, speaks more of a cosmic consciousness that will transcend time with the elimination of our ego at death.[21]

Others, like well-known scholar Paul Davies, see this new science as pointing to a first cause, God. Still others would see it as support for a return to the active God of classical Christianity. They hold that the old mechanistic model was making God appear to be irrelevant. In that world, all God did was to set laws into motion and sit down and watch.

As well as this we need to hear the word of caution from humanist commentator, Bryan Appleyard. He reminds us that, just as the mechanistic theory has been 'proven' wrong, no doubt this new 'weird' science will one day be superseded. Whilst all of us have to rethink our cosmology in the light of the new physics, it would be unwise for any group at this time to base their path on the shifting sands of science.[22]

❖ Insight

Our connecting with Sally left us with a feeling of incompleteness. If all is purely one and we are all part of this impersonal force, where does our capacity and desire to interact with each other come from? And why is it that we have our own personal tastes and dislikes? Further, the whole idea of oneness implies an impersonal energy force, so where does our gift of love come from? The fabric of our very makeup knits us to a framework bigger than cosmic oneness.

In affirming the road to global harmony, there is no need to lose a belief in a Creator-Spirit. This is affirmed by the Sacred Writings where Jesus taught that we can live in a personal relationship with a personal God. Through both the joys and strains of life, there is the abiding comfort of one greater than us whose 'footprints' are alongside ours in the sands of time:

Never will I leave you; never will I forsake you.[23]

5

Sampling psycho-technologies (from A-H):

clairvoyance, fortune telling, holistic healing and others

Healing crystals have been used for thousands of years. They're mentioned in the Bible and by Plato. The pharaohs put lazuli in their head-dresses to clarify the mind. Crystals transfer, hold and also give off energy. Energy is what they're all about; they send out subtle vibes.[1]

We create every so-called 'illness' in our body.[2]

ISOBEL WAS A FREQUENT VISITOR to our stall. She confided that she was a white witch — a neo-pagan devotee. She spoke to us of healing energies that are available. Isobel told us of her personal exploration into these powers. She attuned herself with those mystical, spiritual forces that come from mother Earth.

Isobel said of her partnership with mother Earth: 'What I receive from her, I give back.' To Isobel, we were not truly in line with similar healing techniques spoken of in the Sacred Writings.

In our times together, Isobel explained that the world is out of harmony. She challenged us to break new paths through an intuitive, feminine-based spirituality.

As we talked, it appeared to us and Isobel that, although we had a common commitment to recovery, we might not be soul mates in all the tools we use. Because of our differences, the question of technique was important for our own personal health and inner well-being.

After our conversation with Isobel, we ambled around the New Age festival encountering many practitioners. We saw soul-travel, meditation, tarot cards, books on sacred sex, alchemy, the Holy Grail, yin-yang, mantras, crystals, channelling, holistic healers and much more. These practices were not new to us. Perhaps the most fascinating was the Kirlian photography stall. Via the medium of a photograph, people were shown their aura.

❖ Some psycho-technological tools
At this stage, it might be useful to give a description of how New Agers see these techniques and then explore whether they are, as Isobel suggests, in harmony with those found in the Sacred Scriptures.

❑ *Alchemy*

Although this is popularly thought of as the attempt to turn lead into gold, the alchemical quest is actually a spiritual path to self-purification. True alchemists seek to purge themselves of their moral inner impurities by relying on what is known as the elixir of life, the fountain of youth and the philosopher's stone.

These are concepts and rare substances which enable the seeker to achieve eternal life and purity. The alchemists' chemical experiments are symbols of the internal process of spiritual perfection they are undergoing. Their secret texts on changing the metals from lead into gold are about the inner spiritual realities they encounter. Alchemy is an occult science practised worldwide.

❑ *Auras*

According to many psychics, all life-forms have an 'etheric' or energy shadow surrounding the physical body called the aura. The aura is likened to the halo often drawn in artistic depictions of saints. The aura may be seen through a high frequency electronic photographic technique, known as Kirlian photography. A Kirlian photo shows flares of energy radiating around the physical form. The colours of an aura, it is claimed, can reveal your emotional and spiritual well-being.

Some students of the occult believe that our auras survive for a short time after the death of the physical body and that this accounts for ghosts.

❏ *Channelling*

This is the process of opening up ourselves to a disembodied entity who may speak through us with a spiritual message. This entity could be a departed soul, an ascended master like Buddha, an entity from another galaxy, or perhaps a group entity. Sometimes the channeller needs to enter a trance state in order to receive the message. Others surrender their body and some show little physiological or emotional change.

Another way of receiving messages from beyond is through using a ouija board, where the message is slowly spelled out by a pointer in answer to questions, or by conducting a seance. Possibly the most famous channelled entity is Ramtha. He is said to be a 35 000-year-old warrior from Atlantis, who then went to the Himalayas. Ramtha is channelled by J.Z. Knight and, according to recent reports, is no longer in vogue.

❏ *Clairvoyance*

In the media, the clairvoyant is in much demand. This is a gift which some highly attuned and sensitive people have through which they may foresee the future. It also enables the clairvoyant to have intimate personal knowledge of a person merely by touching an article belonging to them.

❏ *Crystals*

They are at the heart of many delightful tales, including the comic-strip character, Superman.

They are primarily seen as a tool for conducting energy to enhance healing or meditation. Crystals are often worn around the neck or placed in a handbag to generate an even flow of energy. Many experts recommend the frequent handling of your crystal to obtain the maximum benefit.

Evidence for the power of crystals is believed to be found in quartz crystals which produce an electric charge (piezoelectricity). It will produce an electric charge when squeezed. Other exponents claim that the worth of crystals is being asserted by extra-terrestrial beings and UFO contacts.

❐ *Enneagram*
People today enjoy removing the masks that hide their true self. The enneagram assists in this regard. It is a system of classifying and understanding human nature on the basis of a symbolic device (drawn as a circle containing nine equidistant points on the circumference), alleged to have been developed thousands of years ago.

There are nine personality types categorised into three basic groups or triads: the *feeling* triad embraces the helper, motivator and artist; the *doing* triad embraces the thinker, generalist and loyalist; the *relating* triad embraces the leader, peacemaker and reformer. As you ponder on which group you fit into, you discover what personality type you are. It is then possible for you to have an enhanced self-understanding, improved relations with others and be attuned spiritually.

❏ *Firewalking*

This is a popular tool for confronting and conquering fear and proving one's innate powers. It is sometimes used in mind powers programs. The adept strides across a cricket pitch of heated coals without the sensation of pain or injury. Firewalking is also an art practised in many primal societies and is a tour attraction in Fiji.

❏ *Geomancy*

This embraces a number of practices including the conviction that sacred sites such as Stonehenge, Uluru (Ayers Rock) and the Pyramids are part of a large energy grid traversing the planet. Some would see these grids as flight paths for UFOs; they are also believed to be the centrepoints for such global meditation events as what is known as 'the harmonic convergence'.

Geomancy also involves dowsing (using a divining rod to find underground water) and the ancient Chinese art of Feng Shui. Feng Shui is concerned with how one constructs and arranges a house, office or room to ensure a blockage-free flow of cosmic energy and to bring good fortune. For example, practitioners advise that the foot-end of your bed should point away from the door so as to minimise the drain of cosmic energy from the body when sleeping. Similarly, the placing of indoor plants in strategic positions will ensure a maximum, harmonious flow of cosmic energy in a room.

❒ *Holistic healing*

In the past two decades, there has been a trend to move away from orthodox medical practice (with its emphasis on surgery and drugs). People prefer therapies which emphasise a holistic approach to health where their mind, body and spirit are all treated evenly.

Holistic healers emphasise the use of more 'natural' therapies, such as using meditation and herbs. For some, 'herbs' include the extracted oils from flowers, roots, bark and plants (aromatherapy). Lavender makes for a relaxing bath. Healers have also stressed the need for people to develop lifestyle habits which are conducive to health and well-being.

It must be noted that not all holistic healers are necessarily New Age. Some examples of New Age therapies are rebirthing, crystals, astrology, meditation and cosmic energy, which are discussed herein.

Other prominent therapies are:

* *Chiropractic/Acupuncture.* In many classical forms, these therapies purport to tap into an energy force flowing through the body. Illness arises when the energy flow is out of balance.

   D.D. Palmer, the discoverer of chiropractic, believed there was a stream of energy flowing up the spinal column and, by manipulating this energy, he could effect healings. In traditional acupuncture, the imbalance of the flow of energy in your body is said to affect your health. Needles are inserted at key pressure points to reharmonise a patient with this cosmic energy and so restore one's health. This concept of energy (chi) is related to yin-yang which is referred to later.

* *Iridology*. This is a diagnostic system which uses the eye as a map to your internal anatomy and health.

* *Reiki/Therapeutic Touch*. These systems of healing rely upon the healers attuning themselves to your physical/spiritual state and then drawing upon a cosmic energy — sometimes called the Universal Life Force or God — and radiating this energy into your body.

* *Reflexology*. It is believed that the sole of the foot has points that relate to different parts of the body. As the foot is massaged, healing takes place.

❒ The Holy Grail

The search for the Holy Grail was an important quest in medieval European history. It has been made light of in recent years by the amusing comic satirists, Monty Python. The Holy Grail is, of course, said to be the chalice used at the Last Supper of Jesus before his crucifixion. It is claimed that it was carried from Palestine to Glastonbury in England by Joseph of Arimathea, one of the men who buried Jesus.

There are various legends about the grail, particularly in connection with King Arthur. Most centre on a knight who journeyed to a castle, was invited to a feast and there saw the grail. In the myths built upon this story, the grail has been a symbol for power, healing and fertility. As one meditates on the grail legend, the consciousness is quickened by feats of courage. The grail is a potent motif due to its connection with the conquest of death by Jesus.

❖ The value of these tools

The Sacred Writings wholeheartedly uphold the use of spiritual practices for personal and group recovery. This will be more fully dealt with in our final chapter. At this point, however, it is important to reflect on the approaches outlined above.

❑ *Alchemy/Holy Grail*

The Sacred Writings convey the same images of personal transformation which are evoked by the quest for the grail and the alchemist's yearning for purification. A number of early Protestant pioneers, such as Johann Valentin Andreae, saw the fulfilment of the alchemist's quest for the elixir of life, fountain of youth and philosopher's stone in drinking from the eternal wells of salvation provided in the living water: Jesus.

Our sharing with alchemists and grail seekers was to encourage them to let the myth become a symbolic step towards embracing Christ.

❑ *Auras*

The existence of the aura is not inconsistent with anything in the Sacred Writings. When we had our auras taken at the festival, we were encouraged by the advice that we were in tune, and the dominant white rays in the photo around the ears indicated that we were channelling truth!

Auras can be acknowledged as a plausible source for the halo phenomena and ghosts. However, it might be too simplistic to limit ghosts to auras as they *may* be a mind projection or a messenger from God.

One of the most unusual ghost stories concerns the popular translator of Sacred Scripture, J.B. Phillips. Perhaps in a moment of desolation, he had an unusual encounter with the late C.S. Lewis:

> *A few days after [Lewis'] death, while I was watching television, he 'appeared' sitting in a chair within a few feet of me, and spoke a few words which were particularly relevant to the difficult circumstances through which I was passing.*[3]

Could it be that Phillips' tale is similar to the appearance of the 'ghosts' of Moses and Elijah at the transfiguration of Jesus?[4] Whatever one makes of the aura, it is never used as a tool of guidance; rather the dependence is on linking oneself with God.

❒ *Channelling*

The sole instance in the Sacred Writings where there is an actual illustration of channelling is King Saul's visit to the medium of Endor.[5] There, at Saul's request, the prophet Samuel is brought from the other side and he delivers a message of judgment to Saul for using this method of guidance. The implication is that Saul had other trustworthy methods for guidance that didn't require entering the unknown spirit world.

The Sacred Writings indicate that not every spirit is to be trusted.[6] For this reason, as well as losing one's reliance on God, the Sacred Writings forbid our consulting foreign entities. This also applies to the uncertain messages of ouija board games.[7]

□ *Clairvoyance*

One possible explanation for clairvoyance is that some people in their consciousness may be able to live beyond the moment. This may explain ESP and is certainly reflected in prophetic utterances. The concern is when the paranormal is perverted for self-aggrandisement and the vessel seeks to give teachings which are not connected to the Creator's wisdom.

□ *Crystals*

Crystals are referred to in the Sacred Writings in Revelation 21: 18–21, Ezekiel 28: 16 and Genesis 2: 12. The Garden of Eden account states that 'the gold of the land is good; aromatic resin and onyx are also there'. These texts, though, are not saying anything about the power of crystals to change your life. Rather, they are focussing on them for their magnificent aesthetic beauty.

Randall Baer, who died a couple of years ago, was the world's leading New Age expert on crystals. He was a total devotee of the science and wrote the crystal classics, *Windows of Light* and *The Crystal Connection*. He even received visions about crystal-based inventions. These inventions were not confined just to crystals; they also included pyramids, magnets, sonics, New Age music, colour lasers, electronic devices, computers, high-tech trance-induction machines: '. . .I was tapping into what seemed to be a mother lode of New Age sacred science,' Baer said.[8]

However, Baer came to the conclusion that crystals/New Age science is 'the attempt to manipulate reality in increasingly more powerful ways via an occult-based sorcery of sorts'. He leaves us with these sobering thoughts:

> *Is New Age science just another Alice in Wonderland fantasy? Does it involve the placebo effect? Is it a mad scientist's dream? Why are Satan's demons leading more and more New Agers along these lines? Does it have any connection to the UFO issue? These and many other tantalising questions arise about this strange 'Twilight Zone' area of the New Age.*
>
> *No matter whether sacred science works to some degree or no, I can testify today that it is based on occult principles and practices that are all forbidden, either explicitly or implicitly, in the Holy Bible (Deuteronomy 18: 9–12). This is the ultimate flaw of New Age sacred science. It proved later to be one of my most difficult lessons of all to learn.[9]*

❐ *Enneagram*

Practitioners of the enneagram believe that there are

only nine personality types. It can be most helpful and fun to know what our personality type is like — say, melancholic or choleric — but we need to keep in mind we are not limited to the 'boxes' some recovery practitioners place us in.

One commentator has raised some doubts about the enneagram system, suggesting it can open people up to negative spiritual forces.[10] An integrated personality test is the readily available and highly regarded Myers-Briggs Type Indicator, based on sixteen personality types.

❐ *Firewalking*
As a natural explanation, hot coals do not burn flesh without sustained contact. There are those who enter firewalking in an occult spirit of trance and believe that they are being delivered by a super-natural power. As with channelling, the Sacred Writings indicate there is no need to seek God by this fiery path. And, tragically, some have been emotionally damaged as their failure to pass this test has brought a loss of personal esteem.[11]

❐ *Geomancy*
The Sacred Writings affirm the existence of sacred sites and places of power encounters (e.g. Moses at the burning bush). Many people have been nourished by their travels around the fertile crescent's sacred sites. However, the sites are places for Creator worship and personal transformation. They are not springs for cosmic energy grids.

Interestingly, *Time* magazine has recorded that the number of sightings of UFOs — often thought to be connected with energy grids — has diminished since the fall of Marxism in Eastern Europe. Indeed, some UFO advocates are expressing scepticism.[12]

In the case of Feng Shui, the acceptance of our oneness with cosmic energy is not found in the Sacred Writings. Nor is there any guarantee that good fortune will be assured simply on the basis of how furniture is arranged or the position of a doorway.

❒ *Holistic healing*
The Sacred Scriptures speak about healing in many places. They do not go into great detail on the techniques, other than to emphasise the miraculous intervention of God, prayer and sometimes the laying on of hands. The application of natural therapies, such as herbs or traditional procedures, are not specifically addressed by the Sacred Writings. The only caution would be if a healer links your herb with a spirit. We affirm the ministry of the great Master Jesus was one of holistic healing — body, soul and spirit.

There are some philosophies underlying aspects of certain New Age healing that are not as the Bible views the world. One is that illness is purely of our own creation. This view of illness and healing has its base in mind powers and is discussed in a later chapter. There is no denying that much illness is psychosomatic and is related to our own mental well-being and how we see the world. But sickness is not confined to such. For example, bacteria are innocently passed, people accidently fall, there is genetic inheritance and old age.

A consequence of viewing illness as being self-inflicted is that it can create in us a false sense of security. It may also lead to the despair that our illness is because of our own lack of faith. The astonishing end-product of this is found in certain metaphysical groups which claim that all illness is an illusion and the symptoms should be denied. One of the foremost advocates of this was Mary Baker Eddy, the founder of Christian Science.

Another divergence from the Sacred Writings is the notion that there is a unifying cosmic energy which can be tapped into to answer all our problems. As we have already discussed, all is not one and we are not the Divine. Just because your healer gives you testimony of how effective or helpful a treatment has been, this is no guarantee that it is truly right for you. As the Master Jesus taught, even signs and wonders are not limited to the spiritually enlightened. Indeed, some practitioners may be deceived and in other ways mislead you.[13]

We are convinced there is confusion with respect to the healing of chiropractic/acupuncture. Whilst traditionally these practices may be based on energy, many practitioners now accept them as a scientific treatment, even though we don't understand the scientific basis. It has been demonstrated that chiropractic/acupuncture yields results by ministering to pressure points that interact with the whole body. In particular, acupuncture seems to be effective in areas like the thyroid. The fact that how this all works cannot be fully explained to the Western mind is a reminder that the body is a mysterious vessel. Even traditional medicine is not an open and shut case.

❖ Some guidelines in approaching alternative healing

Here are some ideas we have found helpful:

* *Be open to healing.* A wise principle is that nothing is inherently evil and medical alternatives should be explored.
* *Avoid excessive drug treatments.* Our body is to be the temple of the Holy Spirit.
* *Seek healing through natural remedies where possible.* Diet, herbs and relaxation are good examples of this.
* *See diet in the framework of spiritual significance.* Some Sacred Writings references to this are the Feeding of the Five Thousand, Jesus' Last Supper, and the Marriage Supper of the Lamb in Revelation 19: 7–9.
* *Stay in touch with reality and do not simplify the causes of illness.* Disease as an illusion or as the result of my thought patterns are two examples of such over-simplification.
* *Beware of therapies which rely on personal endorsements in the absence of careful testing.* A leading iridologist, for example, failed a laboratory test

when given the opportunity to prove his therapy was valid.

* *Avoid therapists who base recovery on the use of mystical energy.* Be prepared to discuss things with your practitioner and discover his/her understanding.

* *As health is so important, read widely before experimenting with a new therapy.* Test the spirits.[14] A helpful book on the subject is by Swiss physician and psychiatrist Samuel Pfeifer, *Healing at any Price?*[15]

* *If in doubt, leave it out!* This is a useful — and ancient — common sense principle.

* *Go to the master physician, Jesus, in prayer.* This can take place personally, or perhaps you would like to attend a healing service where there is the laying on of hands and prayer in the name of Jesus. We conducted such a ministry at the festival and, as two or three laid hands on the person, there was prayer for their particular complaint and petition that the Lord would deliver them in body, soul and spirit.

Here is a case study of a personal friend of ours who has been marvellously healed. Let her tell her medically verified story which has been featured in our secular media.

Heather says:

In August 1972, while practising the piano, I realised that one of my fingers was stiff. It became sore, red and swollen and I was unable to depress the key. The same thing occurred the following day. I suspected arthritis which tests confirmed as rheumatoid — a strain which I dreaded. Within three months, the arthritis had spread to every joint. For nine months, from midnight to midday, I found it difficult to engage in any activity. Because the pain was worse in the morning, I was advised to give up all morning activity.

I began to experience asthma which was thought to be caused by the medication. . . One of the drugs which kept the asthma and arthritis under control adversely affected me, causing headaches and spontaneous bleeding in the arms and legs, but not in the heart, lungs or brain. To ease the pain, another drug was added. This caused internal bleeding, but after prayer the bleeding stopped and I never bled again. . . Last year my health continued to decline. In April, my bones began to weaken. By February and March this year, I was almost a cripple needing to wear splints.

Heather attended the healing service, even though healing had not been a top priority for her. As a song was being sung, she found herself moved to lay her pain at the cross:

Immediately, I was filled with an intense heat, so great that my skin blistered. During the laying on of hands and prayer, I started to shake violently; then, I felt oil being poured through my body. Within three minutes, my neck pain eased and I could see the ceiling, then the floor. The pain in the rest of my body also eased. The swelling in my joints subsided.

> *Healing is progressing daily. God has no un-*
> *finished symphonies.*

Our journey into other psycho-technologies will
unfold in the following chapter.

6

Sampling psycho-technologies (from M-Y):

meditation, rebirthing, sacred sex and others

Once you begin to embrace who you really are, that is everything that is alive inside you — the dark, the light, the joy, anger, sadness, ecstasy and emptiness — you become more and more sensitive and finally you reach a place where your sensitivity is so refined and so in tune with everything that is, that Tantra begins to happen in lovemaking.[1]

AS WE DISCOVERED in our previous chapter, there are many tools available to us to use in our life's journey. Let's now go on to explore some other aids and then consider their value. As we do, let us keep in mind that many New Age travellers are eclectic and only use those tools which they find useful or appealing.

❖ Some further psycho-technological tools

Here we shall look at meditation, rebirthing, sacred sex, shamanism, soul-travel, sound medicine, tarot cards/fortune-telling, witchcraft/neo-paganism and yin-yang.

❑ *Meditation*

This is a practice common to most religious traditions. The unique emphasis here is on calming the mind from all distractions to enter into a deep spiritual trance and reach a state of inner self-satisfaction. This leads to an awareness of oneness with the universal mind and, through this process of meditation, one discovers one's 'higher self'.

Perhaps the most famous version of this is transcendental meditation, established by Maharishi Mahesh Yogi. He was a guru to the Beatles. He believed the key to the door of meditation was through chanting a 'mantra' and that meditation improved your health and spirituality. A mantra is a sacred word; it may be the name of a Hindu god. A famous mantra is 'Hare Krishna, Hare Krishna, Krishna, Hare, Hare, Hare Rama, Hare Rama, Rama, Rama, Hare, Hare'.

❑ *Rebirthing*

This popular process involves the regression back to the womb, your birth or past-life in order to confront past traumas, rejection, fears and inhibitions. The process often involves a tremendous catharsis of pent-up emotions and sometimes the person releases great anger by punching into mattresses or pillows. The rebirther may use hypnosis or instruct you to use deep breathing exercises to regress back to the womb.

One practitioner, Frank Lake, has suggested that illnesses like migraine, asthma and schizophrenia have their roots in prenatal experiences.

☐ Sacred sex

Watching television today, we easily see that sex is no longer one of the three taboos. There are sex therapists of an ancient spiritual technique known as *tantra*. Yogic exercises are used consisting of a couple trying various sexual postures to awaken spiritual powers. Through the *maithuna* ritual, the couple seeks the suppression of thought, breath and bodily fluid to achieve spiritual enlightenment. The male is said to be Shiva and the female is said to be Shakti.

The couple seek to unlock the *kundalini* or sacred serpent which is coiled at the base of the spine. By various occult techniques in a sexual union, the couple can uncoil the serpent. The serpent rises through various *chakras* — centres of power in the body — until it reaches the crown of the head where the third eye is opened into the spiritual realm. The couple are transformed into a god and goddess, and liberation from the cycle of birth, death and rebirth may be achieved through this sacred sex.

For some who come from the classical tantric tradition, orgasm does not occur, while for others it takes place after the enlightenment occurs. There are various tantric texts which set forth the rituals, exercises and postures.

One famous exponent of tantric practices was Bhagwan Shree Rajneesh and the Orange People. Annie Sprinkle, who was featured in the Australian-made documentary, *Sacred Sex*, says: 'Basically when I'm in a state of sexual ecstasy, that's when I feel a connection with the love, [I feel] all the love of the universe and bliss and the oneness of everything, pure divine love, with God and Goddess and Spirit. Nothing compares to it. To a night where you spend eight to ten hours slowly building and building the excitement and arousal, touching and breathing and baths and sensuality, and you get higher and higher, and higher, and higher and nothing, nothing. . . those are the most blissful moments I know. Nothing compares to that.'[2]

□ *Shamanism*
In primal/tribal societies, there is the figure of the 'holy man' or 'witch doctor' who is a healer, visionary and other-world traveller. The shaman mediates between the spirit world and his tribe.

Shamanism takes many variant forms. It is found in places like Siberia and Korea, and amongst the native North American Indians, Maoris and Australian Aborigines. Shamanism has now been popularised in the West by such visionary occult practitioners as Nevill Drury.

Some also believe in the power of animal totems. The animal can be either a domestic pet or a wild creature.

The animal is a powerful symbol of our link with nature and, for some, a well-spring of guidance.

❏ *Soul-travel*
This is a technique where one can project their soul or etheric body into the spirit world and roam free. Some even talk of astral travel to other continents, planets and galaxies. Soul-travel normally takes place in deep meditation or sleep.

One group that teaches soul-travel is Eckankar. Soul-travel was also popularised in the writings of Lobsang Rampa.

❏ *Sound medicine*
Whether our taste be rock, classical or new vibe, sound and music are major healing components in our lives and universe. Sound medicine takes a variety of forms from our being in tune with the vibrations from the crystals to our having our own healing song, which brings comfort and alters our state of despair. This happens as the healing song brings us into our oneness with the universe. It works effectively with our chakras and mantra chants.

Laeh Maggie Garfield speaks of being able to lie face down to the ground and hear mother Earth's heartbeat. As we get in touch with the rhythms, we will be able to tame an earthquake and direct the growth of plants.[3]

❏ *Tarot cards/fortune-telling*
Who would have thought that shuffling cards

would reveal your future? The tarot consists of seventy-eight cards containing distinct images such as the Magician, the Fool and Judgment. The un-dealt deck of cards is divided into the major arcana of twenty-two trumps and the minor arcana of fifty-six cards.

The term 'arcana' refers to a secret or mystery. The minor arcana is further classified into four suits: wands, clubs, pentacles and cups. For some, these suits represent the four elements: fire, earth, air, water. They stand for our linkage with nature and creation.

The purpose of the cards is to discover what lies in the future and to interpret aspects of your per-sonality. The cards when dealt reveal your underlying motivations and psychological develop-ment. If, for example, you receive the Fool, this could mean you are seeking to be a carefree person. The minor cards when dealt relate to everyday occurrences. Your story comes to life.

Brian McCusker, a retired Professor of Physics at the University of Sydney, and his wife, NDE re-searcher Cherie Sutherland, have conducted 'scientific' experiments using the cards. They posi-tively conclude that 'the cards behave in a way they shouldn't in a materialistic universe'.[4]

Other forms of fortune-telling include numerol-ogy (numbers can be used to predict your future), palmistry (the lines on your hand can be read to predict your future), deck of cards (as with the tarot, a prophetic tool), tea-leaves (the position of tea-leaves in your cup predict things about luck, happiness, family and your life-span) and dominoes (using the numbers on the dominoes to unlock the future).

❒ Witchcraft/neo-paganism

Most witches we know are committed to the neo-pagan way of life. This is true for the modern day Druids who trace their roots to the ancient Celtic world. Neo-paganism stresses the use of the 'old religion' and its reliance upon nature, goddesses, herbs, spells, intuition and oneness with the earth. Authors Aburdene and Naisbitt explain it this way: 'The goddess movement might be termed a mixture of Wicca, the New Age, feminism and mythology. . . present-day witches insist that their tradition. . . is actually life-affirming and based on the power of the female and the earth.'[5]

Many mistakenly accuse neo-pagan witches of being Satanists. In fact, most of them do not believe in Satan. Of course, there are Satanist groups active in our community like the Temple of Set, but these are not part of the New Age or neo-pagan paths.

❒ Yin-yang

From the ancient Chinese religion of Taoism come two important principles concerning the interaction of forces within the universe. It is said that there are equal, opposite yet complementary forces known as yin and yang. These forces are only bi-polar aspects of the one reality, just like the North and South Poles. Yin represents the dark, negative principles, whilst yang represents the light, positive principles.

Harmony within oneself, health, work or the universe is maintained by keeping these complementary forces in balance. Imperfections, illness or disharmony occur whenever one side outbalances the other.

Techniques to maintain the balance between yin and yang are found in Tai Chi, acupuncture, meditation upon the occult text *I-Ching*, or by following the teachings of the Chinese sage, Lao-Tzu. The techniques involve the even flow of energy throughout the universe and ourselves. This energy is often referred to as *chi* and flows from the yin-yang which, in turn, is dependent upon the Tao (the Way).

❏ *Yoga*

This is an ancient Hindu philosophy. This is commonly practised in Western society today. It aims to assist us in breaking free from the cycle of birth, death and rebirth. The word yoga means 'to yoke' or 'to be in union with'. For the traditional Hindu, this union is with the god Brahman.

There are various 'types' of yoga one may practise. Hatha yoga is the best-known because it deals with the various bodily postures people use today as a means of exercise. The postures, however, are not primarily concerned with health or fitness. They are intended to relax the body from all distractions so that the devotee may be enabled to meditate upon a spiritual path.

Another type is siddha yoga. This is concerned with using various 'siddhis' or powers, such as levitation.

In this form of yoga, there are seven major energy centres in the human body called *chakras*. Through various meditative techniques, the practitioner can awaken these energy centres to encounter the spiritual world of the gods and goddesses.

Tantra yoga is a more radical path to liberation which often involves the use of occult powers and sexual rituals (see *Sacred sex*, page 96f above). Raja yoga or 'royal yoga' emphasises the use of body postures, deep meditative trances and mantras to achieve spiritual harmony. Bhakti yoga is a devotional path where one is attached to a particular guru (or teacher) and follows a spiritual discipline combining body postures, meditation exercises, chanting and contemplation of the writings of Hindu sages. The Hare Krishna movement is a well-known example of bhakti yoga.

The essence of yoga is summed up in the philosophical writings of Patanjali, who wrote of yoga as the ultimate path to enlightenment.

❖ The value of these tools
❐ *Meditation/mantra*
Meditation is a valuable technique for growth and recovery. Psalm 1 calls us to meditate and if we do we shall be 'like a tree planted by streams of water, which yields its fruit in season and whose leaf does not wither'. The Sacred Writings call us to focus spiritually on the Creator in our meditation.

The question is whether our spiritual focus will be self- or God-orientated. The answer lies in whether we believe there is a Creator beyond us or whether we are part of a cosmic oneness. If it is the latter, there can only truly be a self-focus as reality lies within us. If it is the former, then self-focus is inhibiting. The potential hazards of going within are that we can lose touch with reality and open ourselves up to all kinds of inner 'voices'.

In the Sacred Writings, we are urged to use the mantra of calling upon the name of the Master: 'For everyone who calls on the name of the Lord will be saved.'[6] Many mantra practitioners move from Creator-praise to losing oneself through the trance-inducing repetition of a divine name. This 'piling up' of deity acclamations in order to find spiritual attunement is discouraged by the Master who says, 'And when you pray, do not keep on babbling like pagans.'[7]

◻ *Rebirthing*

There can be no doubting that many people find the experience of undertaking sessions in rebirthing very helpful to their emotional well-being. In fact, it has been our own personal experience that we have suppressed hurtful events that have only been unlocked many years later. (For those who link rebirthing with reincarnation, we suggest you read our third chapter.)

The Sacred Scriptures understand the value of catharsis. An enthralling case study of this is the famous encounter of Jesus with the woman at the well in John 4. Jesus identified the troubles in her life and offered to heal her past. She declared to her friends and neighbours: 'Come see a man who told me everything I ever did. Could this be the Christ?'

Like ourselves, many pilgrims have found the Christ Catharsis heals. In him, there is a real rebirth. He frees us from human dependency techniques such as hyper-ventilation, found in rebirthing. This is not to deny the essential role and therapeutic value of counselling skills used by those professionally trained in recovery.

☐ Sacred sex

This concept is found in the Sacred Writings, but here it is describing the relationship between a man and a woman eternally committed to each other. Therefore, there is no group sex or voyeurism.

One of the most erotic love poems has been preserved within the Sacred Writings. Life partners would enjoy a time of meditating on it together:

> *Under the apple tree I roused you; there your mother conceived you, there she who was in labour gave you birth. Place me like a seal over your heart, like a seal on your arm; for love is as strong as death, its jealousy unyielding as the grave. It burns like blazing fire, like a mighty flame. . . I am a wall and my breasts are like towers. Thus I have become in his eyes like one bringing contentment. . . Come away, my lover, and be like a gazelle or like a young stag on the spice-laden mountains.*[8]

A good element of tantric sacred sex is the emphasis on learning about each other through touch and exploration. In particular, there is a recognition that males need to develop an intimacy that involves more than sexual intercourse.

In contrast to the tantric, in the Sacred Scriptures sex brings us to praise of *God* for his goodness, not to deification. The ultimate difficulty with tantric sacred sex is its primary goal of self-worship and cosmic oneness. It is inconsistent with Jesus' view of life.

❏ Shamanism

The ultimate shaman of the Sacred Writings is the Mediator Jesus. His unique entitlement is on the basis of his other world journey beyond the grave and return to our realm. He has been to the other side. In contrast, there is no assurance that the other world travels of all other shamans are reliable guides.

Animals remind us of the splendour of creation. There is only one case where an animal is a guide in the Sacred Writings. This is the unusual story of Balaam's ass. This one-off affair contains only trifling insights and nowhere replaces the life-orientating wisdom of Jesus.

❏ Soul-travel

Soul-travel is not directly mentioned in the Sacred Writings. Eckankar maintains that Paul's visit to the third heaven, recorded in 2 Corinthians 12, is an account of soul-travel. Their suggestion is conjecture as even Paul cannot specify how his experience took place. He may even have remained in the body and simply was quickened by the Spirit of God.

John the Apostle's entering into the throne room in the Book of Revelation is in the same category as Paul's vision. Whilst not denying that a miracle is occurring in these people's lives, there is no suggestion that this is soul-travel. It is interesting to note that these apostles' teachings that followed their experiences did not speak of soul-travel.

We have investigated some cases which show trauma can accompany the regular pursuit of soul journeys. Anna is in her twenties and has found the journeys disturbing. She has sought to give them up and even tried a number of spiritual exercises to release herself from them. Yet even now when she sleeps she finds that she loses control of her astral body and is drawn into the labyrinth. It is an uncontrollable torment. We have encouraged her to find release through prayer in the name of Jesus.

❒ *Sound medicine*
Music therapy is a developing science and is particularly useful in assisting the mentally handicapped and those suffering from dementia. It is being constructively used to help women through the stages of childbirth and pacifying children.

Drums, tambour, dance and movement can be used by the client of the therapist to express their frustration, their feelings. Also professionals can use guided imagery. As people relax and listen to music, submerged traumatic images often appear.

We have personally used music as a focus. It motivates, relaxes and allows us to centre our thoughts. In fact, the Sacred Writings acknowledge its role in healing:

> *David would take his harp and play. Then relief would come to Saul; he would feel better and the evil spirit would leave him.*[9]

Music is one of the greatest pleasures of life. Of course, as with anything, it is open to misuse. There is no indication that sound is an absolute means in itself to healing and that it tames nature. Furthermore, there are those who pursue altered states of consciousness, trances and enter into shamanistic journeys by first inducing an atmosphere created by particular kinds of music.

This contrasts with the worship role of music in the Sacred Writings which is to draw us into a conscious, experiential communion with God the Creator and not to 'tune out' spiritually by a loss of our own awareness.[10]

❑ *Tarot cards/fortune-telling*
A.E. Waite, who designed the standard modern Tarot deck, drew his inspiration from the Bible. The Lovers' card symbolises Adam and Eve before God in paradise, and the Devil card shows them after the Fall in chains. The Fool — the most potent and mysterious card in the deck —

stands for a prince from another world whom we do not recognise.[11]

The poet T.S. Eliot in 'The Wastelands' and the novelist Charles Williams in *The Greater Trumps* have drawn upon the deep symbolism of the tarot to point the way back to the salvation story found in Christ. Sadly, most of those who use the cards do so merely a means of peering into the future instead of being awakened to the spiritual truths displayed on the cards. The Sacred Writings critique such an approach, as it moves one's need for guidance from a direct relationship with God to an occult medium:

> *Let no-one be found among you who sacrifices his son or daughter in the fire, who practises divination or sorcery, interprets omens, engages in witchcraft, or cast spells, or who is a medium or spiritist, or who consults the dead.*[12]

Other general forms of fortune-telling seek to answer the deep search for guidance and direction in our world today. The limitation is that they are dependent on human mediums — with all the frailties that implies. It is a Pandora's box. It can be the doorway to foreign spirits.

Fortune-telling can also create a sense of fatalism. A tragic recent example of this was where a father was guided by two fortune-tellers concerning the fate of his marriage. He was told that he would lose his wife and that there would be great tragedy. The man became so despondent that he killed his three-year-old daughter and then committed suicide.

The coroner remarked: 'That's the hazard of going to fortune-tellers who purport to be able to tell your future.'[13]

❐ Witchcraft/neo-paganism

At the festival, one of the most popular stalls was the one selling spells. Spells may work but, as our investigation of these psycho-technologies through the eye of the Sacred Writings has revealed, we are to stop relying on finite magical powers.

The 'old religion' is limited to earth-bound remedies, whilst Jesus trod the higher path. We encouraged our Druid friends to read Stephen Lawhead's novel, *The Paradise War*. It is an enthralling tale of Celtic Britain.

❐ Yin-yang

If we look at ourselves and the world, we see disharmony and imbalances. Our relationships with one another and our own inner sense of well-being suffer from all sorts of stresses and strains. The Sacred Scriptures affirm that we lack balance and harmony both within and without ourselves. We are out of tune with the original order of creation.

However, the yin-yang philosophy of balancing a cosmic energy flow is not found in the Sacred Writings and is at odds with the teachings of the Master Jesus. As we saw in chapter 4, there are drawbacks in basing a path of recovery on this concept of oneness.

❑ *Yoga*
Jesus and the Sacred Writings are in favour of using devotional postures and we explored some of these in our last chapter. Jesus' path, though, was not centred on body postures. His primary spiritual discipline consisted of self-denial and he calls us to follow in his footsteps. In dramatic contrast to the yogic union with an impersonal force, the way of Jesus is to bring us into an encounter with a personal, living God.

*   *   *

As we shared with Isobel about these different kinds of psycho-technologies, her response continued to be: 'I believe that a feminine spirituality is a path of natural wisdom and New Sense healing. By attuning myself with the Mother Goddess of Venus, Isis and Astarte, I have been empowered and transformed. I see the Mother Goddess images as maternal, caring and earth-orientated.'

We empathised with Isobel. She was surprised to hear that there are women today who are finding new meaning and fulfilment in the Christian faith. They are meeting people who are linking their concerns with their spiritual journey. We left each other with the Justin Martyr challenge that we must all leave aside our prejudices and sincerely ask which steps of recovery are truly a blessing.

We reminded Isobel that the way Jesus shared his life with women was revolutionary. *They* were the ones who provided the unbroken chain of evidence as to his death, burial and resurrection. Women were often closest to him in his times of abandonment.

❖ Insight

As our conversation concluded, we reflected on what we had seen and spoken about. Clearly, some New Age psycho-technologies are not inconsistent with the Sacred Writings. Others are. When we pondered this, we asked ourselves why? Those in conflict with the Sacred Scriptures are means for guidance from nature, cosmic energies or such spiritual realms as departed spirits, rather than from God.

It is interesting that in the Bible, especially in the age before the Holy Spirit was given to the followers of Christ, tools were available for personal guidance and recovery. These included dreams (Daniel 2), using a sheep's skin (Judges 6: 36–40), casting lots (Acts 1: 26), Paul's handkerchief (Acts 19: 11–12) and the urim and thummim (Exodus 28: 15–30, 1 Samuel 23: 9–12).

The urim and thummim are fascinating. They were stones the High Priest used to receive a direct 'yes/no' answer from God. However, these tools still differ from New Age psycho-technologies in that they directly bring one to the Divine. In today's parlance, it is like praying about which job I should take and saying to God, as I feel comfortable about all positions, I will accept the first written offer I receive. The letter is like God's confirmation.

In our community, many seek to overcome their hurts and to give fresh expression to their hopes in life. Our authentic pilgrimage must face the dichotomy between the techniques of the New Age and Sacred Writings. Where is wholeness found?

Our admiration for Randall Baer is for a man who has truly known a journey in both worlds. He speaks of his own evaluation and transformation:

> Could all my cherished spirit guides' guidance, all the wonderful mystical experiences, all the sophisticated books that I had read, all the enlightened ones of Eastern mysticism, and all my respected New Age friends' experiences be based on a grand delusion?. . . Everything that I was as a New Ager — everything that I knew I had found, I had accomplished — was now totally up in the air. All things 'New Age' were subject to intense scrutiny in an entirely different way than I had ever scrutinised them before. . .
>
> There are many souls thirsting after truth and feeling the pain of inner emptiness that New Age truth cannot fill. . . Some, so parched with the ultimate dust of New Age 'truth', will joyously accept the Messiah when they hear of him — he who said: 'whoever drinks of the water that I shall give him shall never thirst; but the water that I shall give him shall become in him a well of water springing up to eternal life'.[14]

7

*Healing through Sleeping
Beauty, Atlantis and
other myths*

*At the beginning as well as at the end of the religious
history of man, we find the same yearning for
Paradise.   If we take into account the fact that the
yearning for Paradise is equally discernible in the
general religious attitude of early man, we have the
right to assume that the mystical memory of a blessed-
ness with history haunts man from the moment he
becomes aware of his situation in the cosmos.[1]*

*I began to read American Indian myths, and it wasn't long
before I found the same motifs in the American Indian
stories that I was being taught by the nuns at school.[2]*

GEORGE WAS A VERY OPEN PERSON. He typified the
quest of many today who find meaning in myth. We
believe myths cannot be dismissed as religious fiction,
but rather are stories which give meaning to life.

115

Some myths are created at a particular time and place — they are related to historical events. Others are not. They can come to the surface from within our own being. Joseph Campbell says: 'All the gods, all the heavens, all the worlds are within us. . . Myth is a manifestation in symbolic images, in metaphorical images, of the energies of the organs of the body in conflict with each other.'[3]

'Powerful stories of life's cycle — from my birth, growth, death, resurrection and salvation — are found in common form in all religions,' George told us. And we heartily agreed. We went on to consider other common images like evil, creation and paradise.

George was impressed by the studies of the psychotherapist, Carl Jung. Jung, he stated, had delved into ancient occult texts like the *I Ching*. There, he had uncovered striking symbolic parallels between it and the images found in his patients' dreams. These symbols, which are scattered throughout human civilisation, express the longing for healing, wholeness and integration. For us all, this was a strong pointer to the psychic unity or oneness of humanity.

❖ Sleeping Beauty

One illustration of our spiritual unity which we discussed was the 'Sleeping Beauty' myth. In this story, there is a common body of powerful symbolic images which highlights our need for healing.

There is, for example, the image of the old witch who brings a curse upon an innocent young maiden. The curse involves a prophecy that, when she turns sixteen, she will fall into a deep sleep and no-one inside her kingdom can save her. Be that as it may, another prophecy declares that she will be rescued by a handsome prince who shall come from a faraway land. The prince enters the kingdom through great trials of courage, finds the young heroine and liberates her with a kiss. She is restored and the whole kingdom is healed of the curse.

George went on to highlight the Sleeping Beauty motifs in various spiritual paths: the temptress who brings evil, the helpless victims who suffer, the error of lostness, the champion who brings deliverance, and the Paradise restored.

As we were near the festive season, our thoughts readily turned to Father Christmas. With childlike enthusiasm, we talked about the common tales of Saint Nicholas, Père Noel and Santa Claus.

George's stress, therefore, was that we should explore and embrace the rich mythology of human experience. He invited us to find spiritual reality within these myths. We affirmed that if we open ourselves to the power of myth we can find truth, healing and meaning in life.

We asked George if he would like to chat with us further so we could delve more deeply into these matters and explore other important myths.

❖ **The cosmic tree**
The tree is a popular religious symbol. There is the promise of renewal found in the Christmas tree. The Druids saw the tree as a model of sacrifice. It gave

food, air, wood and shelter. They called it Hu-Hesus. Some Druid devotees find in this name a sign pointing to the sacrificial death of Jesus upon a tree.

In talking with George, we came to the works of the great Rumanian phenomenologist, Mircea Eliade. We discussed Eliade's findings on the image of the cosmic tree which appears in many myths about Paradise. We asked, 'Isn't its enactment found in the Tree of Life in the Garden of Eden?'

George then turned to the cosmic mountain motif where humans ascend to meet with the gods. Our thoughts were drawn to Moses on Mount Sinai.

We pointed out to George some of Eliade's insights into the ritual of cannibalism.[4] Eliade wrote of the Uitoto cannibals who experienced the whole of life as a dance. Their rituals continually reminded them of the pristine primordial paradise. They believed partaking of human flesh connected them with the first human assassination that took place in this Utopia. Here, we drew George to the account of Cain and Abel which speaks of such a primordial assassination as one brother slew another.

All of us agreed that the works of Campbell, Jung and Eliade on myth are a signpost to our basic unity — or, as Jung termed it, the 'archetypes of the collective unconscious'. We ourselves stressed that the Sacred Scriptures indicate that all humanity comes from the same stock. So we should not be surprised to discover that we have common dreams, needs and aspirations. As the Sacred Writings say, 'From one person God made all nations who live on earth.'[5]

Mention of Jung raised a growing concern that scholars have. Their apprehension is that people like Jung have fallen for the fallacy of *absolutising* myth. For example, the fact that Jung's body of patients had common mythological symbols in their dreams does not mean one can read this into the history of every religion.

A good illustration of this is the pole myth that appears in many communities. There is a pole that links the world to the heavens and sometimes this pole is broken and needs to be restored. A few have sought to impose this myth on the Australian Aboriginal religion when it is not there.

❖ The horned creature myths

Another common tale in religious experience relates to the personification of evil. The fact that this myth has a real cosmic reality is documented in the writings of current secular historian, Jeffrey Russell. He has penned five seminal works: *Lucifer, Satan, The Devil, Mephistopheles* and *The Prince of Darkness*.

Russell argues that the only way to make sense of our universal experience of cosmic evil is to acknowledge the existence of a cosmic being who has poisoned human affairs. He surmises:

> *If the Devil does exist, what is he? If the concept has any meaning at all, he is the traditional Prince of Darkness, a mighty person with intelligence and will whose energies are bent on the destruction of the cosmos and the misery of its creatures. He is the personification of radical evil, and he can never*

be irrelevant because humans have always sought to understand and to confront that evil. That search, that need, is a sign that meaning is there, however obscurely it seems to be hidden from the intellect. . .

It is easier to go the Devil's way with hatred and violence and indifference. But the Devil's way not only is morally wrong; it is stupid. It will never work; it has never worked. Violence always provokes violence; hatred everywhere provokes hatred. Daily, we are reminded that we have not yet learned this. The Devil stands like a blind man in the sun, seeing only darkness where he stands among the brilliant green fields of God's creation.

We have thought the Devil's way long enough. It is time for a new way of thinking.[6]

This adversary has been represented in the medieval European images of the great figure of Satan and has been present since time immemorial. One of the earliest Christian images is of Christ ransoming us from these spiritual bondages: 'For God has rescued us from the domain of darkness and brought us into the kingdom of the Son he loves.'[7]

❖ Atlantis, Lemuria and Paradise

At the festival we found people asking, 'What about Atlantis?' The original story for Atlantis, of course, is found in the writings of Plato. The modern interest in the Atlantis story comes from the writings of I.T. Donnelly and is further popularised by Shirley MacLaine. Donnelly saw it as a super-civilisation of advanced technology and occult knowledge that gave birth simultaneously to the Egyptian and New World cultures.

Anthropologists like Irving Hexham have shown that there is no evidence to suggest Egypt and the New World had a common parentage. They had different languages, racial groups, technical developments, crops, medical insights, domestic animals and culture. Hexham speaks of these claims about Atlantis being historically false.[8]

Another potent lost continent saga concerns Lemuria (also called *Mu*). Some claim it sank into the Pacific having once linked Japan with America and Oceania. Other occultists believe it connected Africa and India to Australia.

Charles Leadbeater was a prominent theosophist who believed that a remnant of Lemuria was to be found amongst the Australian Aborigines. If this is true, then the Aborigines would be the ancestors of our modern civilisation. These occultists who believe in Lemuria imply that the secret spiritual practices of this lost continent are not fully expressed in the continuing Aboriginal traditions. One possible exception would be the spell of the tribal shaman pointing the bone. Despite this loss of Lemurian practices, they encourage us to learn from the Aborigines' attachment to the land.

Early European explorers groped for lost paradises in the uncharted parts of the world. Tales about lost continents such as Ponce De Leon's fountain of youth, the mythical kingdom of Prester John, as well as Sir Thomas More's *Utopia* inspired these quests. Those who followed in the wake of Columbus went west to the Americas in search of paradise.

Many more believed there was a great southern continent that was special to the heart of God and our human journey. Thus the Spanish explorer Pedro de Quiros set out to find 'the Great Southern Land of the Holy Spirit'. The hopes of the Spanish, Portuguese and Dutch of finding this virgin paradise of the southern hemisphere were put to rest by James Cook.

In modern times, the common utopian myth inspired Marxists to building a new world uncorrupted by human evils. Their golden age of a classless society soured under the repression of the Soviet bloc behind the Iron Curtain.

❖ The nourishment of myth

Modern society no longer has the unifying framework that traditional cultures have enjoyed. For example, the Australian Aborigines have lived by their 'Dreamtime'. The stories of the Dreamtime have provided a context for meaning and a way of living in the world, whereas in our highly urbanised, technological society we lack such a unifying fabric. Alvin Toffler, in his *Future Shock*, describes our dilemma through the adventures of a young wife:

> *When you live in a neighbourhood, you watch a series of changes take place. One day a new mailman delivers the mail. A few weeks later the girl at the check-out counter at the supermarket disappears and a new one*

takes her place. Next thing you know, the mechanic at the gas station is replaced. Meanwhile, a neighbour moves out next door and a new family moves in. These changes are taking place all the time, but they are gradual. When you move, you break all these ties at once and you have to start all over again. You have to find a new paediatrician, a new dentist, a new car mechanic who won't cheat you, and you quit all your organisations and start over again. It is the simultaneous rupture of a whole range of existing relationships that makes relocation psychologically taxing for many.[9]

John Naisbitt, in *Megatrends*, likewise strikes out at our modern anxiety by noting:

Helped by the news media, especially television, we seem to be a society of events, just moving from one incident — sometimes even crisis — to the next, rarely pausing (or caring) to notice the process going on underneath.[10]

The sense of disturbance in our mobilised technological society calls for the unifying framework of myth, folktales that can be passed down from generation to generation.

One 'yarn' or folktale that has broad application is the story of the Prodigal Son. It can be paraphrased as follows:

A father has two sons and the younger asks for his freedom. The father gives him his share of the inheritance and the son goes and squanders it all in a foreign state. He finds himself lost and alone finding shelter in a pigsty. He plucks up courage and returns to his father, expecting at best to be received as a servant. His father, who has never lost his love for his son, sees him from afar and races to embrace him. The son who is lost has returned and is received into the family. Sadly, the elder brother finds it difficult to accept the one whom the father has forgiven.[11]

In this story, we see the universal experience of mobility, lostness, greed, abandonment and rejection. It speaks of our ache for healing, understanding and unconditional love. Such tales of recovery found in the Sacred Writings can undergird a person, family and community.

We also invited George to rediscover the tales of Tolkien and C.S. Lewis. Tolkien spoke of our encounter with folktales. The climactic event or rescue which occurs in these stories Tolkien called the '*eu*catastrophe' — a joyful happening:

The Gospels contain. . . a story of a larger kind which embraces all the essence of fairy-stories. . . The birth of Christ is the eucatastrophe of man's history. The resurrection is the eucatastrophe of the story of the incarnation. This story begins and ends in joy. It has pre-eminently the 'inner consistency of reality'. There is no tale ever told that men would rather find was true, and none which so many sceptical men have accepted as true on its own merits. For the art of it has the supremely convincing tone of primary art, that is of creation. To reject it leads either to sadness or to wrath.[12]

As we shared with George, we came to a mutual understanding that common myths are at the heart of religious experience. The Master Jesus put flesh on the myth.

❖ Insight

One of the sad aspects of some contemporary Christian scholarship is the attempt to remove the 'myth' of incarnation, miracle and resurrection from the scriptures. The justification for this action is that such myths are not perceived as culturally relevant to modern society. Such reductionism leaves one with a faith with no heart or mystique.

The barrenness of modern life without any 'myth' is highlighted by the popular hunger for folktales by such authors as Stephen Donaldson, J.R.R. Tolkien and C.S. Lewis. What is also quite poignant is that surveys are showing that those Christian communities which retain the core myths are the ones that are growing. Some have suggested such growth is related to their being fundamentalist in theology. Maybe rather it is due to their retaining a message that sparks the inner consciousness of people.

Whilst affirming with George that religion contains common myths that are available to be embraced in Christianity, we felt the need to stress one vital point. We explained that myths like Sleeping Beauty have an actual objective base. They are not just good internal realities, but are historical encounters. The champion (Master Jesus) actually did come into our dimension to rescue the princess (us) by a kiss (the cross) and restore paradise (heal our lost, soul-sorrow lives). This brings a unique light to the Sacred Writings.

All these myths testify to our universal longing to return to a 'lost' paradise where we have peace, harmony and unity with one another and God. In *The Aquarian Guide to the New Age* we have this description of Atlantis:

> *Running halfway along the entire length of the island was a fertile coastal plain. Some miles away, in the centre of the island, was a low mountain, possibly little more than a hill, on which developed the island's most ancient city. This city was surrounded by three moats, traditionally built by the god Poseidon. There was abundant vegetation and animal life, much of which seems to have been tropical in nature. There was mining for a now unknown ore, orichalcum, described as 'more precious than anything but gold.'[13]*

In Christ, the myth has become reality and awaits its consummation:

> *Then I saw a new heaven and a new earth, for the first heaven and the first earth had passed away, and the sea was no more. . . And I heard a loud voice from the throne saying, 'See, the home of God is among mortals. He will dwell with them as their God; they will be his peoples, and God himself will be with them; he will wipe every tear from their eyes. Death will be no more; mourning and crying and pain will be no more, for the first things have passed away.'[14]*

8

Using the mind's power and our human potential

Your mind creates your reality. You can choose to accept this or not. You can be conscious of it, and get your mind working for you, or you can ignore it, and allow it to work in ways that will hinder and hold you back. But your mind will always, and forever, be creating your reality.[1]

I am learning to alter my perceptions and therefore change my 'reality'. . . This was not easy when a mugger lunged at me on First Avenue with the clear intention of doing whatever he deemed necessary to get my handbag. I remember my flash reaction that I, by God, did not like playing the part of a victim. Instinctively I changed my 'part' and lunged back at him, shrieking like the Wicked Witch of the West until the mugger thought my insanity was something he didn't want to tangle with. I changed the script.[2]

> *Jesus said, 'Everything is possible for him who believes.'*[3]

AS WE WANDERED AROUND THE STALLS, we came to a 'mind powers' exhibition. We were looking at the posters when Charlie, a young executive type, came up to us. He sketched for us an overview of the state of mind people exist in — 'unconsciousness'. He defined this as using only ten per cent of your mental powers. We agreed that most of us under-use our mind.

Charlie then spoke on how we can be empowered to operate on a higher level of consciousness. If we enter into this altered state of consciousness, we will be guaranteed profound enhancements in our work, relationships, life's goals and religion. Charlie's salesmanship was an enthusiastic endorsement of what this had done for him.

We asked Charlie how we could enter into this higher state of consciousness? He explained that this could be done through participating in his program. It was ultimately about equipping us to realise our mind creates our reality. We write our own life's scripts. He was one who accepted karma from a past life as influencing one's script. There were others who only focussed on the present. Some devotees added that we will only achieve what we desire when we find we are one with the unlimited, creating Universal Mind. The Universal Mind is whatever you perceive God to be.

Our conversation with Charlie returned to a

fairly earthy, base level. We mutually felt the need to reach the bottom line of his philosophy.

Ross: Charlie, are you saying that through our mind we can be totally in control of our destiny and your program could allow us to achieve that?

Charlie: Yes.

Ross: If I desire a new relationship, can I mentally create it?

Charlie: Sure.

Ross: If it failed, would it be my own fault?

Charlie: In the sense that you have allowed yourself to have that experience. Probably you must have it for your own growth.

Ross: And that would be true for the failure of my own small business? The recession is not the problem, but my dream?

Charlie: Yes, I guess that has got to be the bottom line.

Philip: Charlie, I realise it's an extreme example, but I want to explore the depths of rescripting. I'm Hitler reincarnated. Knowing what my karma is likely to produce, I come to you for guidance. How do I recreate this life's path through mind control? Could you help me?

Charlie: You wouldn't know you were Hitler.

Philip: No, I've just been to the clairvoyant next door who has informed me that I was Hitler in my previous life.

Charlie: Oh. I don't think I can answer you.

> [Charlie found this a difficult scenario, so we returned to perhaps more current examples.]

Ross: Charlie, there is one place in the world where we would not expect to find a mind powers program operating. That is in the refugee camps that darken our globe.

> [Charlie did not deny this. We had one last puzzle.]

Ross: Charlie, there is a four-year-old starving in Ethiopia. A victim of world apathy, oppression, poverty or their own visualisation?

Charlie: It's basically their choice.

❖ Mind powers players, principles and stated benefits

There has been a remarkable spread of different organisations employing mind powers and human potential theories. Some of these groups are not as doctrinaire as Charlie. Still, their emphasis is that we have to 'get it' — as we think, so we are and we are responsible for our own lot.

These organisations include: The Forum, Insight Transformational Seminars, Silva Mind Control, Pacific Institute, Foundation of Human Understanding, Supercamp and Winners' Camp. They offer their services to the business world, education, sports, armed services and the general community.

The principles employed by these players are:

(a) Creative visualisation
This is where you learn to create by the power of

thought your own desired reality, such as envisaging winning an Olympic Gold Medal. You believe your thoughts have materialised in the physical world.

(b) Self-hypnosis

This involves training yourself to go deep within your mind to tap into your subconconscious creative powers.

(c) Neurolinguistic programming (NLP)

There are said to be three forms of communication between humans and these relate to three learning styles. Some are good listeners and learn well by hearing (auditory learners); others see things better and learn by demonstration (visual learners); while still others learn by doing things (kinesthetic learners).

As well, by reading a person's body language (such as eye movements, gestures, postures and other non-verbals), you understand how to communicate better. It aids you in assessing someone's character by the style and choice of words they use.

Its creator, Richard Bandler, says that NLP 'teaches people to run their own brains instead of letting their brains run them'.[4]

(d) Centring

This is a technique designed to harmonise your 'left brain' (your rational, analytic side) with your 'right brain' (your intuitive, creative side). This is done by using relaxing music, meditation and breathing exercises.

Charlie passionately emphasised the blessings of mind powers. He underscored these benefits as: greater productivity and creativity in the workplace, control of stress, removal of illness, reduction of blood pressure, increased efficiency, enhanced ability to study, better lovemaking, peak performances and the certainty of winning.

The Eternal Flame Foundation espouses earthly immortality as being a fruit of mind powers. Whilst this might appear to be a bizarre claim, it is a logical outworking of mind powers concepts. They claim death brainwashing is fed into us from the time of our birth: 'from an ancestry that accepted death as inevitable. The truth is our bodies are beautifully and wonderfully designed and without limitation.'[5]

❖ Superlearning

At the festival, we also met a number of parents and teachers who work to transform education through a process they call 'Superlearning'. We gathered that it draws on a variety of theories, principles and practices to enhance learning and memory retention. During the 1960s, George Lozanov of Bulgaria experimented with new ways of learning. He found that by combining yogic breath exercises with the 'beat' of classical music playing in the background, his students could learn foreign languages in a matter of weeks. They believe that tone and language go hand-in-hand.

Lozanov's pioneering studies have developed a more New Sense direction in the West. This is apparent in Supercamp, Winners' Camp and Discovery. Some participants told us how they were encouraged to improve their self-image and no longer view themselves as failures. They were shown how to apply meditation, creative visualisation, self-hypnosis, neuro-linguistic programming, centring and New Age techniques to their studies. We listened to the praises of some thirty parents and pupils who claimed that these programs had powerfully transformed them.

The creator of Winners' Camp and Supercamp, Eric Jensen, in his book *Superteaching*, unfolds the recent emergence of the right brain/left brain concept. Jensen looks at the two hemispheres of our brain. Some suggest there are two centres which relate to our analytical (left brain) and intuitive (right brain) capabilities. Jensen aims to produce a wholly integrated student who can master his mind. To do this, we must focus on the creative right brain as too much stress has been placed on the left brain.

Our experience has confirmed that contemporary education tends to be analytical at the expense of the creative. Still, Jensen's approach reflects a love of the intuitive as against the logical and is sacrificing a balanced learning pattern by over-emphasising the right brain. Many educators believe that holistic education involves both reason and creativity, whether it be in the area of maths, language or spiritual studies. It is a *both/and*, not an *either/or* area.

One process of mind powers that surfaces in education is values clarification as a foundation for a healthy mind. This concept, which can be quite helpful, calls for teachers and educators to assist pupils identify their own values.

However, at times a dogma emerges in this process. Some educators instruct their pupils that there are no absolute values, that life is purely about finding your own values and accepting other people's views. That in itself is a New Age value statement. We wonder how such educators would respond to a classroom comprising bigots, misogynists and those whose values have been formed by hurtful childhood experiences. Is our motto to be 'What I do is right' or 'I do what is right'? The former idolises self-discovery.

❖ Caring sharing companies

It is common for major corporations to utilise mind powers workshops for the benefit of their staff. Not satisfied with corporate henchmen, companies are hunting for creative, confident visionaries.

The impact of this influence was shown when a major newspaper consulted us in the course of their research into mind powers. Their article was concerned with employees being forced to participate in these workshops.[6] Some of the distinguishing marks of these New Age business seminars are:

* visualisation is the key to success
* positive affirmations where one engages in self-congratulations
* the use of psycho-technologies (like mantras, rebirthing, soul-travel) as a means of reducing stress
* the promise of unlimited success
* large payments to attend the courses
* secrecy or reluctance to reveal the content of the seminars to their clients prior to staging them
* long hours spent over a short period of time
* in some seminars there is a strong component of emotional confrontation designed to shatter one's preconceptions and self-image, in order to reconstruct you into a truly enlightened person. Werner Erhard's EST programme was noted for this, with statements like 'Your life doesn't work!'[7]

These recessionary times also find some businesses relying on tools like astrology for their motivation and planning. Newspapers even carry horoscopes for businesses. Other companies consult clairvoyants. In the midst of this pursuit for survival and profit, there is as well the industrial chaplain who works alongside employees in the company as a care-giver.

❖ Reach for the sky
Charlie was intrigued to find that the Sacred Writings disclose that we are the pinnacle of creation and are in the image of God. Job chapter 28 reveals

our wisdom, vision and ability to explore even the depths of the earth for minerals. We travel into realms beyond the reach of the greatest bird or beast. We shared how the Sacred Scriptures encourage us to have a healthy self-image as we are loved by the most significant Person in the universe. With God on our side, nothing is impossible!

We shared with Charlie that the Sacred Writings have a threefold practical emphasis which departs from his understanding of mind powers. First, we do not control everything, nor are we necessarily responsible for our predicament. We interact with forces and circumstance and suffer from the actions of others. We are interconnected. We simply do not create all our destiny by thought. The story of the Good Samaritan tells how an innocent man was waylaid by thieves. What happened to him was not his fault.[8]

He put to us a Bible text that Louise Hay often cites: 'As he thinks within himself, so he is.'[9] 'Isn't this speaking of mind control?'

We replied: 'The verse in the passage where it is found refers to a stingy-minded person who acts as a dinner host. He is obsessed with the cost of the meal. What the proverb is saying is that such a person will only give you scraps. This is not advocating mind control, but giving us a warning: Beware of Scrooges!'

Charlie was a step ahead of us and was ready to pounce on our second point. 'I suppose you are now going to tell me that there is a God up there who orders and sustains everything.'

We responded: 'That's how we understand the world. We've had some tremendous personal experiences where God has clearly guided us. For us, Jeremiah speaks the truth, when he says: "Before I [God] formed you in the womb, I knew you; before you were born, I set you apart."'[10]

Finally, we turned to servanthood. It is not about mere words like 'change your script', but involves deeds and costly action. In the story of the Good Samaritan, two religious characters avoided the victim, but the Samaritan reached out. Jesus saw servanthood as the ultimate path to wholeness:

'Which of these three do you think was a neighbour to the man who fell into the hands of robbers?' The expert in the law replied, 'The one who had mercy on him.' Jesus told him, 'Go and do likewise.'[11]

We canvassed with Charlie whether it is not servanthood that makes a person, family, business, team and nation 'great'. Isn't the true identity of Australia, for example, seen in the ANZAC spirit?

❖ Pat your dog and dig in your garden

Charlie reminded us that we live in a stressful world. What techniques beyond mind powers can we discover to handle stress?

We joked about two of the best-known 'bush' remedies. One is to pat your dog. Our pets are a kind of in-house therapist. The second is go dig in your garden. Professional health-care workers tell us these really do work. (We can personally testify to this with respect to the dog! They relieve tension and aggression and produce a state of relaxation.)

Apart from these homely remedies, the Sacred Writings give at least six basic insights:

(a) Have balanced goals

Don't get uptight about material things. Jesus said: 'Therefore I tell you, do not worry about your life, what you will eat or drink; or about your body, what you will wear. Is not life more important than food, and the body more important than clothes?'[12]

(b) Give yourself space

Jesus in his own hectic times would say, 'Come with me by yourselves to a quiet place and get some rest.'[13]

(c) Confront the hurt

Paul was a model in coming to grips with what emotions, people or situations were causing him stress. He would identify the cause and positively confront it. In his various letters, he identifies undermining spirits and seeks to tackle the problem.[14]

(d) Don't keep anxieties to yourself

Healing and strength are often found in opening ourselves to trusted friends and/or professional helpers and talking the issue through. As the life song of the Travelling Wilburys echoes, 'Everybody got somebody to lean on.'

As Galatians 6: 2 connects: 'Carry each other's burdens.'

(e) Be aware that God cares
Jesus said: 'Look at the birds of the air; they do not sow or reap or store away in barns, and yet your heavenly Father feeds them. Are you not much more valuable than they?'[15]

(f) Trust the power of prayer
Paul the apostle of Jesus writes: 'Do not be anxious about anything, but in everything, by prayer and petition, with thanksgiving, present your requests to God. And the peace of God, which transcends all understanding, will guard your hearts and minds in Christ Jesus.'[16]

❖ Fallen stars
It now seemed opportune to discuss with Charlie some 'yin journeys' we were privy to of devotees of unlimited mind powers programs. These stories show the potential for psychic disturbance that can come through an uncritical experimentation with roads to recovery.

❑ John
John attended a mind powers course with his wife. They came to the conclusion that business success and riches awaited them — all that was necessary was to reprogram their thought patterns. They could do it! In a time of recession, they reached

out into small business and even overstretched. Their belief in what was told to them became a wellspring of enthusiastic banter.

Some six months later, John was sharing over lunch his brokenness. His wife had determined that she could visualise a better partner and had left him. The business had collapsed and he was facing bankruptcy. He had left some primal beliefs in a personal God behind when he embraced mind powers. He now believed there was no-one to walk beside him in his pain. The false hope of reprogramming had left him alone and broken. As psychologists tell us, unrealised and unrealistic expectations are the seed-bed of depression.

❒ *Andrew*

Andrew is a young sports psychologist who faced the dilemma of the role of mind powers in sport. He saw the role for dreaming and mental preparedness. For example, on a bad day rehearsing a golf shot in one's mind. It helps with coordination. However, the absoluteness of mind powers troubled him. But he felt some pressure to inform his clients of this technique.

He used as an example of the problem six people in the final of a major athletic race. Each has been counselled by team assistants in a basic mind power technique. They have been told that the race victory they have visualised is truly theirs. One, of course, fulfils his ambition, the others do not.

Andrew asks, 'Who is ultimately going to take

responsibility for the disappointment and heart-break of the losing finalists? And how will this shape the everyday decision-making processes of the six athletes?'

❒ *Kathy*

Kathy was diagnosed as having a malignant tumour. In counselling, she was encouraged to see the tumour in her hand and pass it to the healer. She was reminded that, as she created the tumour, she was the one who could let it go. Therefore, to ensure that the cancer had been removed, she had to deny its existence no matter the pain or its sense of constancy. Whilst the counselling sessions were couched in religious terminology, in reality healing depended on her faith in her own mind.

Kathy did not improve. The family's frustration reached the extreme that anybody who was not positive in their vibes and outlook was kept from her presence. She eventually died and the family lived in uncertainty and agony.

❖ **There are no accidents**

The notion that you write your own script can lead to some unrealistic, unhelpful and disconcerting ends. In *The New Age Catalogue*, we have the following explanation of AIDS:

> *When it is no longer necessary to have a disease such as AIDS upon the earth plane, when no-one needs that experience anymore, then someone from the Spirit*

side may very well pass the idea to someone on the earth plane and a so-called 'cure' will come forward. But there will always be some other illness waiting in the wings, some other way to exit for the human being who is choosing to leave the earth plane. Cures come when the disease is no longer necessary. There are no accidents. As long as there are those who need to have the experience of leaving the Earth by AIDS or have the need for the communication of AIDS (and changing their lives because of it), it will stay upon the earth plane. Always. Those within the Spirit dimension will not interfere in any way with the earth plane. It is always the choice of those on the Earth as to their needs and their path.

As more and more individuals go within and discover their own inner guidance, work on themselves, take responsibility for their own lives, then less and less is there need for what some would see as catastrophe or tragedy. There will be those who choose to leave through Earth changes, volcanic eruptions, airplane crashes, all forms of departure. And when there is no further need for those experiences, then there will be no further need for that illness or experience to be manifest and it will go away.[17]

During our time at the festival, we interacted with various New Age leaders. Chris James is a marvellous musician and singer. His theme song based on the poetry of Wordsworth means much to us: 'We are angels, we have forgotten these things; trailing clouds of glory, we are remembering.'

After one of his performances, we discussed spiritual journeys. We asked him: 'How do you explain that there are victims in this world whose despair is not of their own making? What about the refugee?' His response was that these sorts of conundrums are for the philosopher or theologian to work out. His calling is to focus on the positives. We appreciated that. But we still posed the question: 'If your world-view has a substantial Achilles heel in it, is it not time for a new paradigm? Can we hide in the positives whilst some who are savaged by injustice are chained to crushing circumstances?' He understood our concerns.

❖ Insight

As we have mentioned, there are positive aspects to mind powers. All of us have benefited from positive thinking. The concern with the modern mind powers movement is its unrealistic view of thought *alone* creating reality. Here is an instance of its strengths and weaknesses.

Robert is a young man whose outlook was radically changed through participating in a mind powers forum. He took responsibility for his fractured family relationships and his diminished achievement in his university studies. Yet he discovered a self-centredness and a total self-dependence in mind powers. Although he was helped in part by the workshops, he had reservations about who he was becoming and the world view he was adopting. He transcended the negatives through embracing the positive life of Jesus. There, he found servanthood and a purposeful relationship with the Divine.

We agreed with Charlie that there is a new consciousness percolating in our midst — one we wanted to own. It is an altered state of consciousness not bound by the shackles of falsely programmed patterns of thought. The new human is lateral, positive, balanced within and harmonised with the environment. The new human steps confidently into the future.

We suggest the following affirmations for the new human which integrate the insights of mind powers and the Sacred Writings. They reflect an empowered mind in tune with the realities of life:

* *We affirm that transformation/refocussing your goals begins with the renewing of the mind.*
* *We affirm that we are special, created in God's image — and have been given tremendous capabilities.* We will positively use our gifts, intuition and creativity.
* *We affirm that we are dependent on circumstances, others and God for life's fulfilment.* This is a beautiful concept and is in touch with reality.
* *We affirm that we are a shamrock of body, mind and spirit.* We only operate as a wholly integrated person when energised by the One who is beyond us, yet who is near enough to personally comfort, guide and strengthen us.
* *We affirm that life is more than thought and involves*

adventure even beyond our own creativity.
* *We affirm that love is more powerful than dreams.*
* *We affirm servanthood and dying for others is the authentic path.* We conceive people, families and nations growing together in mutual service.

In 1989, the Canberra Raiders Rugby League team were facing their greatest challenge. Grand final day was upon them and they had yet to win the cup. Although the team was physically prepared, it lacked inner drive.

We are involved with a group which is responsible for placing chaplains in professional sporting teams. Our chaplain to the Canberra Raiders, the Reverend John Woods, handed a personal letter to the captain of the team. He does not believe that prayer wins football matches, but sensed it had a life of its own. The press would later report that this letter had been a motivating force for many of the players. As a goal was kicked that tied the game, and as a victory try was scored in extra time, the key players kept in mind the chaplain's words.

Our chaplain wrote:

Just a note to wish you and the other guys all the very best for Sunday. I consider it a privilege to have been associated with you as Chaplain over the years. These sentiments would be echoed by your families, friends and many thousands of Canberra fans. Simply stated, the Grand Final is a challenge for you to realise your God-given potential as footballers.

Inside each of you is a dream. Dreams do come

true if you are willing to sacrifice what you are to become what your dream calls you to be. My prayer for you is that of St Paul: 'May your hidden self grow strong.' May it be a great game played in the true spirit of the occasion.

Good luck, God bless and see you Sunday.

We shared with Charlie that this letter does not embrace simple mind powers. Rather there is an interconnecting between our dreams, God and service to the game. We also shared the stories of some international sports figures who have found that true greatness comes from who you are, not what you have achieved. And that greatness is ultimately a gift from God. We offered Charlie a copy of Ross' book *The Gods of Sport* which tells these stories in detail.[18] As our time together came to an end, we were all left pondering whose path was truly life-enriching.

9

Searching for Jesus' missing years

*Of course, the 'truth' about the missing years in Jesus'
life cannot be historically proven and, therefore, will
always be subjective for each individual who explores
it — which is the way it should be. We have no
need to prove anything about this story.*[1]

*Christ travelled through many countries teaching and
performing all kinds of miracles before arriving in
Judea to teach the doctrine formulated in Japan. This
provoked the Romans who sentenced Jesus to death
by crucifixion, but Jesus' brother, Isukiri, voluntarily
sacrificed himself on the cross.*

*At the age of thirty-six, Christ went on a four-
year journey to northern Europe, Africa, Central
Asia, China, Siberia, Alaska, down through both
Americas and back to Alaska. He then arrived at
Matsugasaki Port in Japan (now part of Hachinohe
in Aomori Prefecture) on 26 February in the 33rd*

year of Suinin, together with many followers from all countries he had visited on the way. Christ's final years were spent at Herai, where he died at the age of 118.[2]

When they had gone, an angel of the Lord appeared to Joseph in a dream. 'Get up,' he said, 'take the child and his mother and escape to Egypt.'[3]

COLIN WAS A VISITOR to the festival who wanted to connect with fellow travellers in the search for meaning. He was in his mid-forties and a passionate genuine seeker. He raised with us some interesting points about the life of Jesus. He had read Paramahansa Yogananda's *Autobiography of a Yogi*, where Jesus' wisdom is said to have come from the Hindu scriptures.

Like so many others, Colin had also seen the television documentary, *The Lost Years of Jesus*. This film suggested that Jesus spent his missing years — between the ages of thirteen and twenty-nine — studying and preaching in India, Kashmir, Nepal and Tibet. Colin said that there were actual scrolls in Tibet which told of Jesus' travels to these places in Asia. He challenged us to go beyond the limitations of the Bible and to embrace these other scrolls. There, we would find the full teachings of the great master.

In our little booth at the festival, we were to talk a lot with many 'Colins' about international travels of Jesus. This subject is one of the most interesting and mysterious to explore. It was stimulating to talk to those who were trying to get in touch with the true Christ.

Apart from the locations mentioned in our introductory quotes, Jesus is said to have travelled to countless other places including Greece and Persia.[4] C.C. Dobson cites myths of trips to Stonehenge.[5] The Sacred Writings indicate that Christ did go beyond Palestine — he at least found his way to Egypt as a child.

What is the documentary evidence for Jesus travelling to all of these other places? The fact is the evidence is slight. This does not worry people like Janet Bock, who stress that Jesus' travels are based on subjective insights.

The weakness with this approach is that history is recast as romance that fits our own hidden fantasies. It is just as valid for us to see Cleopatra and Mark Antony embracing on the sandy shores of Sydney. Such subjective imaginings might at times enliven our dreaming, but have no bearing on our understanding of what influenced Jesus.

❖ Jesus in Tibet

The focus of the historical material for these international travels is Nicholas Notovitch's *Unknown Life of Jesus Christ*. Notovitch was a Russian journalist who visited India, Kashmir and Tibet in the 1880s. When he visited a Tibetan Buddhist monastery, the head abbot told him how the great master Jesus was honoured in one of their own scrolls.

According to the abbot, Jesus (known to them as

St Issa) came to India and Tibet during his early years and studied the Vedas and Buddhist sutras. Once he had mastered these sacred writings and their spiritual practices, he went back to Palestine to preach. Notovitch asked if he could be shown these scrolls, but the abbot was reluctant to do so on that occasion. He told Notovitch that, if he ever revisited the monastery, he would be allowed to look at the scrolls.

As fate would have it, Notovitch left the monastery but was thrown from his horse and broke his leg. Since the only safe place was the monastery, he was brought back there and, whilst recuperating, he was granted his wish. The abbot would sit with him reading the stories about St Issa as Notovitch made notes. Later, Notovich arranged them in the format of a biblical book. He was to report such incidents as this:

> *In his fourteenth year, young Issa, the Blessed One, came to this side of the Sindh and settled among the Aryas, in the country beloved by God. Fame spread the name of the marvellous youth along the northern Sindh, and when he came through the country of the five streams and Radjipoutan, the devotees of the god Djaine asked him to stay among them.*[6]

Notovitch went on to publish the story of his travels, including the new 'Gospel' document he had discovered. It first appeared in French in 1894 and in English shortly thereafter.

Two later major works which show a literary dependence upon Notovitch are Levi's *The Aquarian Gospel of Jesus the Christ* and Elizabeth Clare Prophet's *The Lost Years of Jesus*. Prophet's work is a recent defence of the whole Notovitch saga. And she documents other teachers, such as Swami Abhedananda and Nicholas Roerich, who later went to the same monastery and claimed to have seen the scrolls. Their publications vary only slightly from Notovitch's work.

Elizabeth Clare Prophet's book has photos of books with this caption: 'These books say your Jesus was here.' Sadly, one can't read the photographed manuscript. At present, Clare Prophet has an underground bunkered community in the forests of Montana where her followers are awaiting a cataclysmic war.

As one can imagine, the sceptics quickly followed in pursuit of Notovitch's work. One initial response came from the comparative religion scholar, Friedrich Max Müller. In deference to Notovitch, he thought that he may have been the victim of a practical joke by the Buddhist lamas. Müller expressed his opinion in the popular British journal, *The Nineteenth Century*.[7] Notovitch in a fresh English edition responded to Müller's article with this challenge: 'Let it even be proved to me that I am wrong.'

Scholars took up Notovitch's challenge. Archibald Douglas was a professor at Government College in Agra, India. He had no axe to grind, but decided to spend his vacation retracing Notovitch's steps. Douglas wanted to view the scrolls for himself.

In 1895, he arrived at the same monastery that Notovitch had referred to. Douglas was accompanied by a translator who interacted between himself and the head abbot. In dialogue form, the following was asked:

Q: Have you or any of the Buddhist monks in this monastery ever seen here a European with an injured leg?

A: No, not during the last fifteen years. If any sahib suffering from serious injury had stayed in this monastery, it would have been my duty to report the matter to the Wazir of Leh. I have never had occasion to do so.

Q: Have you or any of your monks ever shown any *Life of Issa* to any sahib and allowed him to copy and translate the same?

A: There is no such book in the monastery and during my term of office no sahib has been allowed to copy or translate any of the manuscripts in the monastery.

Q: Are you aware of the existence of any book in any of the Buddhist monasteries of Tibet bearing on the life of Issa?

A: I have been for forty-two years a lama and am well acquainted with all the well-known Buddhist books and manuscripts, and I have never heard of one which mentions the name of Issa. It is my firm and honest belief that none such exists. I have inquired of our principal lamas in other monasteries of Tibet and they are not acquainted with any books or manuscripts which mention the name of Issa.

Q: M. Nicholas Notovitch, a Russian gentleman who visited your monastery between seven and eight years ago, states that you discussed with him the religions of the ancient Egyptians, Assyrians, and the people of Israel.

A: I know nothing whatever about the Egyptians, Assyrians and the people of Israel, and do not know anything of their religions whatsoever. I have never mentioned these peoples to any sahib. . .

(I was reading M. Notovitch's book to the lama at the time and he burst out with, 'Sun, sun, sun, manna mi dug!' — which is Tibetan for 'Lies, lies, lies, nothing but lies!'. . .)

Q: Is the name of Issa held in great respect by the Buddhists?

A: They know nothing even of his name; none of the lamas has ever heard it, save through missionaries and European sources.

Douglas concludes:

I have visited Himis, and have endeavoured by patient and impartial inquiry to find out the truth respecting M. Notovitch's remarkable story, with the result that, while I have not found one single fact to support his statements, all the weight of evidence goes to disprove them beyond all shadow of doubt. It is certain that no such passages as M. Notovitch pretends to have translated exist in the monastery of Himis and therefore it is impossible that he could have 'faithfully reproduced' the same.[8]

It should be noted that Notovitch made no response to Douglas' report and in fact disappeared from the stage.

Elizabeth Clare Prophet does not let the matter rest. She suggests that the lama may have been reluctant to be upfront with Douglas as he wished to protect his scrolls. She speaks of the others who have journeyed to Himis and viewed the scrolls. The problem is that she paints the lama as a liar of convenience. Also, not one of the other travellers has publicly supplied any photo, parchment or Tibetan copy to verify their story. All they give us is their own translation of an unseen document.

Apart from Douglas' research, the greatest obstacle to Notovitch's story is the fact that Buddhism did not reach Tibet before the seventh century AD. As the Buddhist, Christmas Humphreys, notes in his standard introduction to Buddhism:

Before the seventh century, the sole religion of Tibet was the Bon (i.e. Shamanism). . . Some time in the fifth century AD, a number of Buddhist books were brought into Tibet from India, but they seem to have been ignored, and it was not until the reign of King Srongtsen Gampo, in the middle of the seventh century, that Buddhism became a force in Tibet.[9]

There was simply no Buddhist monastery in Tibet for Jesus to visit.

Then there is Notovitch's linguistic problem. He claimed that the scrolls he saw were translated into Tibetan from the sacred Pali language. The fact of the matter is that no Buddhist literature of Tibet was ever translated directly from Pali. The Pali language was confined to southern India and Ceylon.

Other problems with the scrolls Notovitch translates are:

* He refers to the Jains (Djaines) as believing in God. The Jains, however, do not believe in the existence of any God!
* The spelling of the document contains nineteenth century anachronisms, such as Nepaul for Nepal.
* Notovitch and others claim that the document is the most reliable and accurate source from the first century AD concerning the teachings of Jesus and the Bible. In reality, the scrolls speak of many Jewish temples in Palestine, but archaeology establishes there was only one in Jerusalem.
* In the first edition of his book, Notovitch claims to reproduce a single scroll. However, in the second edition, in answering Max Müller he writes: 'The truth, indeed, is that the verses of which I give a translation. . . are to be found scattered through more than one book without any title.'
* Jesus is supposed to have mastered Buddhist teachings. A careful reading of Notovitch's

work shows that there is no real resemblance between Buddhist dogmas and what is upon the lips of his 'Christ'.

❖ Jesus in India

A number of modern day gurus such as Yogananda, Sai Baba and Bhagwan Shree Rajneesh believe that Jesus travelled to India. They appear to base their knowledge on Notovitch and/or subjective intuition. One who goes further is Edgar Cayce, who in his trances 'tapped' into psychic records in the spirit world known as the Akashic Records. These records apparently talk of Jesus' Indian journey.

A passage that is sometimes referred to by these teachers is Luke 4, verse 22 which indicates that the hearers of Jesus were amazed at his wisdom, asking, 'Where did a carpenter's son gain such insights?' Could this not be proof that he must have gone to India? This is not the answer disclosed in the Gospels. They indicate that Jesus was wise because he was God incarnate and, if he had any assistance, it was from the Holy Spirit. Such a person would not be dependent on earthly guides.

There is a further problem. Whilst Jesus acknowledged the wisdom of the ancient writings in the Old Testament, he never spoke of the Vedas, Sutras or Tantric materials. Nor do we see Jesus using the postures of hatha yoga or Buddhist prayer chants in the Gospels. If he travelled to the East, surely he would have shared these insights with his disciples and encouraged them to seek such learning.

Another matter which should be borne in mind with respect to the influences upon Christ is that he lived in a Graeco-Roman world. Most scholars find his concepts and phraseology relying on his Jewish culture and his Graeco-Roman world rather than on any supposed Japanese, Tibetan or Indian influences.

A small Muslim sect known as the Ahmadiya have a variant story of Jesus coming to Kashmir after the crucifixion. In his book, *Jesus Died In Kashmir*, A. Faber-Kaiser offers a reconstruction of what occurred. Jesus did not die on the cross, but survived and fled to Kashmir with his wife Mary Magdalene. It is believed that the lost tribes of Israel are the ancestors of the inhabitants of Kashmir. Jesus' tomb is claimed to be in Srinagar. They claim to have Christ's footprints in stone, his tomb and a living descendant.

Leading scholar Per Beskow, Associate Professor of Patristic Studies at the Swedish Council for Research in the Humanities and Social Sciences, maintains the Ahmadiya claim is based on the faulty Notovitch work.

Paul Pappas, Professor of History at West Virginia Institute of Technology, takes the matter further:

> *Although the Ahmadis claim to have the tomb of Jesus in Srinagar, India, no historical evidence has been offered to confirm its authenticity except for questionable works based on oral legends. In addition, the Ahmadis have failed to produce any archaeological or anthropological evidence that the grave. . . might*

be that of Jesus. Therefore, the Ahmadi thesis is based only on the revelation of Hazrat Mirza Ghulam Ahmad, the founder of the Ahmadiya movement.[10]

One result of the Indian pilgrimage stories is that some have now combined the Notovitch claim with the Ahmadiya claim, so that Jesus makes two visits — one before his crucifixion, one after. The *National Geographic* reflects this influence and further responds to the Notovitch tale:

When we were in Srinagar, we were told of a book written by a European (Notovitch) who advanced a strange theory. The author claimed to have found documentary evidence in Himis that Jesus Christ had been to Ladakh in his lifetime.

After the crucifixion, so the tale goes, Christ was not buried in the Holy Land, but was brought secretly to little Tibet, brought to life by Himalayan herbs and later ascended to heaven from the Himalayas. We were also told that this author mentioned going to Himis and seeing the document with Father Gergen. But the venerable old gentleman (Father Gergen) assured us he knew of no such evidence. Though he remembered the author, he had never been to Himis with him.

After reading the book, several European church dignitaries wrote to Father Gergen asking for corroboration and details of this matter. When we visited Himis, we asked about the document (Notovitch's scrolls), but the lamas didn't know what we were talking about. It was Greek to them![11]

❖ Jesus in Japan and France

In recent times, attention has been placed on the 'Kirisuto Legend' which speaks of Jesus arriving in Japan at the age of twenty-one and spending ten years studying Shintoism. He returned to Judea to proclaim these teachings, but was opposed and his brother Isukiri was crucified in Jesus' place. Jesus then left Judea and returned to Japan at the age of thirty-seven and died at the age of 106 years. His tomb is said to be in Herai where one can see a signpost erected which outlines the legend. This claim has been extensively promoted within the New Age, Japanese-based group, Mahikari.

Another controversial claim has come with the book, *The Holy Blood, The Holy Grail*. The authors claim that Jesus survived on the cross and revived in the tomb. He then took his wife Mary Magdalene out of Judea and probably settled in France. The Merovingian royal dynasty, they claim, was the direct blood-line from Jesus.

In his book, *The Case for the Empty Tomb*, co-author of this book, Ross Clifford, analyses whether a man who had been subjected to torture, flogging, the cross and a spear-thrust to the side could appear a couple of days later as large as life. He would have to pretend to have conquered death for the 'myth' of resurrection to have survived. We agree with the sceptic Strauss that such a scenario is a greater miracle than the resurrection itself! As for someone taking Jesus' place on the cross, this would make him out to be a complete fraud. This is inconsistent with his character and status.

As to Jesus being married to Mary Magdalene, there is simply no evidence for this.

So, the Japanese and French accounts are based on legends. There is little, if any, historical base that you can check.

❖ Jesus the Essene/Gnostic

Colin wondered: 'Well, what about the possible links between Jesus and the Essenes and Gnostics? Could these paths, rather than the eastern-mystical spirituality, have been Jesus' guiding light?'

We shared with Colin that the Essenes were a Jewish group probably known to most through the famous Dead Sea Scrolls, whilst the Gnostics are associated with such writings as *The Gospel of Thomas*.

The Dead Sea Scrolls bring fresh insights into the Jewish religious scene before and around the time of Christ and for this we must be most grateful, as they help us better understand the world in which Jesus lived. The Scrolls were found near Qumran on the Dead Sea in 1947. They deal mainly with the life of a particular Jewish sect in the last two centuries BC. These scrolls, though, make no mention of Jesus, John the Baptist or any other New Testament figure.

An Australian scholar whom we have studied under and respect greatly is Dr Barbara Thiering. She is almost alone in her endeavour to link Jesus to the Dead Sea Scrolls and the Qumran community. Her latest book, *Jesus the Man*, has caused some sensation.

A couple of points need to be borne in mind. The first is that Barbara Thiering is not New Age and would be horrified to find any such connection. Second, there is no documentary evidence to directly link Jesus with the Scrolls. She relies on her own 'pesher' method — i.e. finding the hidden meaning in the text — to reconstruct the history of the early Christians. Third, she follows the path of theologian Paul Tillich who holds that religious statements are purely symbols pointing to something beyond themselves.

From this position, it is hardly surprising to find that she has reinterpreted the Gospels and the Dead Sea Scrolls to fit a meaning not found on the surface. Most scholars of a variety of academic backgrounds, those with and without faith, have dismissed her theory about Jesus and the Scrolls.

Finally, the Dead Sea Scrolls themselves do not speak of any cosmic consciousness, karma and reincarnation. Neither do they relate to any of the Hindu or Buddhist scriptures.

The Gnostic gospels are fascinating to study. Some of these books pick up various sayings associated with Jesus and some speculate on the hidden aspects of his life. A large collection of the Gnostic writings were found at Nag Hammadi in Egypt in 1945 in a jar in a Graeco-Roman cemetery. The problem with relying on these documents is we are most uncertain as to their date, authorship and reliability as records. They fail the basic historical tests set out below and just cannot stand up to Matthew, Mark, Luke and John. To rely on the Gnostic books is like riding a bike when one is able to travel in a Ferrari.

Some venerate the Gnostic gospels in the sense that they place great stress on sayings which are not found in the traditional Gospels. Yet, a striking contrast between the Jesus of the Gospels who constantly affirms women is found in the final saying of the Gospel of Thomas. 'Peter' argues:

> 'Let Mary [probably Mary Magdalene] go away from among us because women are not worthy of the life.' Jesus responds, 'See, I shall lead her, so that I will make her male that she too may become a living spirit, resembling you males. For every woman who makes herself a male will enter the kingdom of heaven.'[12]

Such an aversion to womanhood is hardly admirable. Some try to redeem the Gospel of Thomas by suggesting this saying is a later addition. The problem still remains in that it represents the thought of a Gnostic devotee.

As Colin listened to our views on Gnosticism and the Essenes, he asked for our opinion on New Age writer, Edmund Bordeaux Szekely. We were aware that Szekely claimed he had discovered a previously unknown text, called *The Essene Gospel of Peace*. Szekely was of French-Hungarian descent and was concerned with promoting a vegetarian lifestyle.

Szekely insisted that he had discovered fragments of an Aramaic manuscript at Monte Cassino, Italy, in the mid 1920s. Two more substantial versions were said to be found, one in Old Slavonic held at the National Library of Vienna and the other in Aramaic held in the Vatican's archives. According to Szekely, Jesus was an Essene who believed in a Heavenly Father and an Earth Mother.

We read:

> *It is by love that the Heavenly Father and the Earthly Mother and the Son of Man become one. For the spirit of the Son of Man was created from the spirit of the Heavenly Father, and his body from the body of the Earthly Mother. Become, therefore, perfect as the spirit of your Heavenly Father and the body of your Earthly Mother are perfect. And so love your Heavenly Father, as he loves your spirit. And so love your Earthly Mother, as she loves your body. And so love your true brothers, as your Heavenly Father and your Earthly Mother love them.*[13]

We put it to Colin that to be a devotee of Szekely is a troublesome journey. No-one has been able to find the manuscripts which Szekely said he had found and translated in Vienna and Rome. Scholars such as Per Beskow have stated they should be easy to locate if they exist.[14] Further, Szekely was reluctant to assist anyone in their search for this truth and supplied no catalogue or other library numbers. Szekely alone has read them.

❖ Jesus' various travels

Colin asked us, after our discussions over the various travels of Jesus, why not accept this multiplicity of journeys? We pointed out a major stumbling-block: it would have been impossible for Jesus to have travelled, studied and died in all these various places. A lot of the stories contradict each other, so one has to ask which story is true.

It is enriching at this point to apply basic historical criteria to the various stories of Christ. This is something we have found many New Agers enjoy, as they like to get to the core of the Jesus path. Ross has documented the way to do this in *The Case for the Empty Tomb*. Briefly, there are three criteria:

1. *The transmission test*

Has the written document been carefully and reliably copied and recopied from one generation to the next? As we don't possess any of the original documents with respect to Jesus' life and journey, we must check the process of copying in the available manuscripts. In the case of the New Testament books, there are more than 5 000 Greek manuscripts which one can peruse to check on the copying process. And when the copies are compared, they complement each other so that an original can be faithfully reconstructed. None of the other 'lives of Christ' in any way pass the test.

As scholar R.T. France has said of the varying lives of Jesus:

All such reconstructions of Jesus necessarily have in common an extreme scepticism with regard to the primary evidence for Jesus, the canonical Gospels, which are regarded as a deliberate distortion of the truth in order to offer a Jesus who is fit to be the object of Christian worship. Instead, they search out hints of 'suppressed evidence', and give central place to incidental historical details and to later 'apocryphal' traditions not unknown to mainstream biblical scholarship, but which have generally been regarded as at best peripheral and, in most cases, grossly unreliable. The credulity with which this 'suppressed evidence' is accepted and given a central place in reconstructing the 'real' Jesus is the more remarkable when it is contrasted with the excessive scepticism shown towards the canonical Gospels.[15]

2. *The internal test*

Do the documents claim to be written by eyewitnesses or by those closely associated with the witnesses to the events recorded in them? In the case of the biblical books, both Matthew and John were written by eyewitnesses to the events, while Mark's Gospel is believed to comprise the preaching of St Peter. Luke's Gospel begins by acknowledging that he has carefully checked things out with the original eyewitnesses:

Many have undertaken to draw up an account of the things that have been fulfilled among us, just as they were handed down to us by those who from the first were eyewitnesses and servants of the word.

> *Therefore, since I myself have carefully investigated everything from the beginning, it seemed good also to me to write an orderly account for you, most excellent Theophilus, so that you may know the certainty of the things you have been taught.*[16]

The other stories on the life of Jesus, *if* they have inspectable documents, do not have the eyewitness testimony. They tend to be legendary in form and speculative in nature.

3. *The external test*

Is there any data outside the documents to confirm their claims or contents? With the biblical books there are numerous archaeological remains, inscriptions and sociological material to confirm their general details. There are also Graeco-Roman and Jewish historical writings (such as Tacitus, Josephus, Pliny the Younger) which correlate with the Gospel records.

In contrast, we have noted above how Notovitch's work is inconsistent with external data with respect to names, places and language.

So we shared with Colin that, when one looks at the stories of the various journeys of Jesus, there is only one about which there can be any certainty. This tells us that Jesus was a refugee child in Egypt, that he lived, died and rose again in Palestine. We accepted we all have an inclination to embrace the mysterious tale rather than settle for the trustworthy but sometimes incomplete historical narratives. We also explained that Gospel investigation was not simply a matter of dredging through crusty old books, but was also something of an existential reality. We illustrated this with the following case study.

We encountered John at a New Age seminar we were conducting inter-state. At the end of the seminar, there was a time for story-telling. John shared that his life had been desperate and he had found no strength or meaning in his journey into his inner self. In fact, he was at the point of no return. He decided to take one last astral travel.

In this journey, he encountered a bright light that he could not look upon. He then heard a voice which he recognised as one who had comforted him when he was sick in his youth. The voice said: 'You have encountered the Godhead. You cannot look upon it. Go back into your body and read the Gospels.'

He read the Gospel of John and he found that it transformed his life. It self-authenticated itself to him. He stood up in the power of the Spirit as a new disciple of the great Master, Jesus. 'Read them [the Gospels] for yourself,' he pleaded, 'and by so doing encounter the real Jesus'.

❖ Embrace the traveller

We said to Colin: 'Suppose that Jesus really did journey to India and other places. Would that not only add credence to his followers' assertion that he is the enlightened one? He must truly be the Master of all wisdom. Before him, of all the ancient sages, we must truly bow.'

Of himself, Jesus says this is who he is and why he had come:

I tell you the truth, I am the gate for the sheep. All whoever came before me were thieves and robbers, but the sheep did not listen to them.

I am the way, the truth and the life; no-one comes to the Father except through me.

I am the resurrection and the life. He who believes in me will live even though he dies.

I am the bread of life. He who comes to me will never go hungry, and he who believes in me will never be thirsty.

For even the Son of Man did not come to be served, but to serve and to give his life as a ransom for many.[17]

It was Thomas the doubter who fully expressed the magnitude of Christ when he said to the resurrected Jesus, 'My Lord and my God'.[18] Rhineland medieval mystic, Meister Eckhart, has put it nicely:

The greatest good God ever did for man was that he became man himself. Here I shall tell you a story that is relevant to this.

There was once a rich man and a rich lady. The lady had an accident and lost one eye, at which she grieved exceedingly. Then the lord came to her and said: 'Wife, why are you so distressed at losing your eye?' She said:, 'Sir, I do not mourn because I have lost my eye. I mourn for fear you might love me the less.' Then he said, 'Lady, I love you.' Not

*long afterwards, he put out one of his own eyes
and, going to his wife, he said: 'Lady, so you may
know I love you I have made myself like you. Now
I, too, have only one eye.'*

*This is like man, who could scarcely believe that
God loved him so much, until God put out one of
his own eyes and assumed human nature.*[19]

It is apparent that we know little about Jesus' life
between the ages of thirteen and twenty-nine years.
The Gospels are silent. The temptation has been to have
him journeying to other countries to find wisdom.

As we shared with Colin, the straightforward
explanation for these years is that Jesus was
sanctifying the ordinary. When Luke speaks of
Jesus growing in wisdom, no doubt he simply
means that in his life as a child, student, carpenter
and adult he learned how to appreciate the ordinary
things of life — just as we must do.

As his Jewish ancestor wrote in Ecclesiastes: 'One
can do nothing better than to eat and drink and find
satisfaction in work. This, too, I see is from the
hand of God.'[20] From this mastery of the ordinary,
Jesus has been able to relate to all. That is why he
lives on.

❖ Potholes to transformation

Colin by his words and movements was signifying
his openness to Jesus. There were, however,
potholes in the road to recovery in Christ — not
academic potholes, but ones that touched his very

being, stumbling blocks that we ourselves had agonised over, genuine concerns that penetrate the very nature of faith.

He took his first step. 'What about those who haven't heard about Jesus? Is it fair that they miss out on eternal life simply out of ignorance?' We shared with Colin that there are a number of differing views on this matter. The scriptural view, in our opinion, is that we are judged on the basis of the light we have received and not on the revelation we have not received.[21] In other words, as Romans 1 makes clear, all know of God and his attributes. Those who have not heard of Christ will be judged on what they know of God. Still, we encouraged him to place his faith in Christ. After all, who would want to stand before God on their own karma?

His second pothole related to sin. He found the concept obnoxious. Was he really that unacceptable to God? We answered by asking whether sin wasn't really the best explanation of the human predicament. Don't we feel that at times we fail ourselves, others and the One beyond us? How else do we make sense of the anger, hurt and hatred in the world? Has not sin been with us since time immemorial? Simply to see wrongdoing as an illusion or a step for correction is not to do justice to the human cry for forgiveness and cleansing from guilt.

We explained to Colin that a lot of our interaction with New Agers has been with respect to sin. They have revealed they just cannot 'positively affirm' away the dark side of their inner being and community life. We concluded by pointing out that Jesus takes the sin problem seriously. When he hung on that cross, he did what we could not do — he paid the price for our sin. In him is the positive affirmation that I am liberated from sin.

On the matter of sin, Colin focussed the discussion on one of the best-selling New Age writings on Jesus, *A Course in Miracles*. The book purports to be channelled teachings from Jesus given through the 'vessel' of Helen Schucman. The text comprises three parts: the first contains the messages from Jesus; the second is a workbook for students; the last part is a manual for teachers. The book has impacted in a major way, to the extent that Jerald Jampolsky has popularised the essence of the course in his own sought-after book, *Love is Letting Go of Fear*.

Colin pointed out that *A Course in Miracles* has no negative concept of sin. In his view, it expresses the words of Jesus. For example:

No-one is punished for their sins and the Sons of God are not sinners.[22]

All our sins are washed away by realising they were but mistakes.[23]

Our concern with the Course was that, although it is at times an inspiring piece of literature, it has four drawbacks:

* *It is a recent channelled work and, unlike the historical Gospels, there is no verification that it carries the words of Christ.* If it does not, then it is the message of a deluded spirit guide.

* *It is inconsistent with what we do know Jesus said.* A good instance of this is seen where, in the Course, Jesus tells us: 'The Holy Spirit dispels [guilt] simply through the calm recognition that it has never been.'[24] In John 16, verse 8, Jesus taught, 'When he [the Holy Spirit] comes, he will convict the world of guilt in regard to sin and righteousness and judgment.' If Jesus is a great guru, one cannot live with two inconsistent statements.

* *It is not in touch with life.* As we have discussed in this book, evil, suffering and wrongdoing is simply not overcome by positive thought. The world is more complex.

* *Some have found that the course is detrimental to their spiritual journey.* A case study on Genise in the *SCP Journal* provides this insight:

> *During this time, I counselled and rebirthed many people. They thought I was a very wise person, because I could tell them about the Course. It sounded so profound. But I knew in my own heart that the Course was not helping me get over my hurt. I still felt resentful and unforgiving. For me, the Course was guilt-producing, rather than guilt-releasing.*[25]

None of the Course's affirmations were working in her life and she wasn't being allowed to deal realistically with the hurts in her life.

We prayed that Colin would discover the filling in of his 'potholes' — that he would freely walk the path of Jesus.

❖ Insight

We agreed with Colin that we live in an age of disharmony. The world is hurting through unemployment, recession and family breakdown. People feel isolated in an age of mobility — orphans in a cosmic universe. In an age where the political wall between East and West has been torn asunder, the human heart throbs for inner peace, healing and a community reconciliation that is more than a redefining of national barriers.

The question we asked of each other is: 'What is the first step of recovery?' It must focus on finding the teachings of One who can lead us to a real understanding of ego and our place in the world.

This spiritual desolation is typified by the nation of Russia. On a humanitarian visit to that land, we discovered a system which for seventy years had relied purely on material factors. It is now searching for a spiritual vitality to bring the country out of the depths of the abyss Marxism had produced.

An important woman for us is Svetlana Titik, former Deputy Justice Minister for the Republic of Russia and now the Director of the Gorbachev Foundation. Svetlana came in touch with us through our writings and we sat down as friends and spoke for some hours. The question she asked we heard again and again throughout Russia: 'Whom can we trust? We cannot trust the human leaders of this world as they have continually let us down.' We replied that she could trust the Master Jesus and with this she concurred.

In our own spiritual desolation, we ask the same question: 'Who can bring us transformation? Whom can we trust?' Do we trust the stars, our past lives, other earthly gurus, myths, crystals, spirit guides, mind powers and the unsubstantiated Jesus of the New Age? Or is the first step to recovery trusting the One who said he was God and proved it by his resurrection from the dead? The One who offered more than words for salvation in that he gave his own life. The One who has given the greatest ideal for living — servanthood. The One who is unique in comparison to all other religious leaders and gurus, still reaching into the here and now and touching our lives through the Spirit. *Whom* do we trust?

Our conversation with Colin deeply moved us all. He acknowledged that the reconstructed stories about Jesus' many travels left him with many questions.

We shook hands as new friends learning together in the journey of life. He shared that he was going home to read the Gospel stories — to let Jesus speak for himself. He was on the threshold of genuine Christ consciousness.

10

Finding the door to transformation

All I really need to know about how to live and what to do and how to be, I learned in kindergarten. Wisdom was not at the top of the graduate-school mountain, but there in the sandpile at Sunday school. These are the things I learned:

> *Share everything. Play fair. Don't hit people.*
> *Put things back where you found them.*
> *Clean up your own mess. Don't take things*
> *that aren't yours. Say you're sorry when you*
> *hurt somebody. Wash your hands before you*
> *eat. Flush.*[1]

I am convinced that, by their nature, children live in Dreamtime. Most parents are given children as their spiritual directors.[2]

Anyone who will not receive the kingdom of God like a little child will never enter it.[3]

THE GRAND CLIMAX of the festival was the oneness celebration on the main stage. There, many of our new-found friends were dramatising the fulfilment of the New Age dream of universal unity and harmony. The stage was alive with the tribal rhythm of drums, didgeridoos, dancers and harmonic singing, and decorated with totems, banners and lights. The scene was electric!

There were Aboriginal people, Maoris, Native American Indians, gurus, pilgrims, healers, inquirers, sceptics, meditators, the authors and officials all together 'holding hands' and affirming their commitment to a New World Order.

This spirit of New World Order is reflected in politics, in the festival participants and in the teachings of the great Master, Jesus. Within the human heart is a common yearning for peace and brotherhood. On the eve of the twentieth century, many anticipated the realisation of this dream through liberal humanistic endeavour. It was sadly crushed by the horror of the slaughter of fellow human beings in two world wars.

The failure of this earlier search can be summed up in the thoughts of Tolstoy who implied that everyone is trying to change humanity, but no-one is trying to change the heart.

The new global vision will not live beyond tomorrow unless the heart is the centre of our focus. From changed hearts there is an evolving, changed world. Contemporary Russia and the failure of Marxism is another witness to the need for a value system and philosophy that transcends the material.

What follows is a list of our affirmations based on the teachings of the Master, Jesus. They are progressive, beginning with one's higher self and consummated in a global vision. They seek to take one out of soul-sorrow, a sense of alienation and disconnectedness and bring us to an understanding of ourselves. They, like the rainbow, stand for a new day. They are based on the premise that meaningful life today is found in simplicity.

As a barrister who was a mentor of ours used to cackle, 'Keep it simple, stupid!', or when he was feeling more eloquent: 'You annoy me when you confuse yourself!' Life today is about the basics, uncovering the child within.[4]

❖ Tools to attain your transformation
Our affirmations are as follows:

❒ *Positive connections*
We affirm the discipline of prayer. It is our way of talking to God. We live in a day characterised by the multiplication of humankind's machinery and the diminution of God's power. The great preoccupation of our day is work, work, work! The new battle-cry is: 'Organise, organise, organise! Give us some new society! Tell us some new methods! Devise some new machinery!' But the real need of our day is encounter with the living God — and this is achieved supremely through prayer.[5]

Sometimes it's a struggle. This was understood

by Spanish mystic, Teresa of Avila. She spoke of the four degrees of prayer. She likened them to various ways in which a garden is irrigated. The first way, drawing water out of a well, is a hard slog where we appear to be relying on our own capacity. The last is rain, where one is overwhelmed by the showers of divine energies.

Prayer that touches us like rain is often enhanced by our postures. The Sacred Writings mention these: kneeling (a sign of homage, emptiness and earnestness), hand movements (raised hands, spread-eagled hands, palms turned upward are signs of worship and that we are not closed to the Divine blessing), eyes raised and open (a sign that we are focussed on the celestial realm and the strength and power therein), body work (a sign of our emotional status through drama, such as beating our breast). Passages that help us learn more about prayer postures are Ephesians 3: 14, Philippians 2: 10, Luke 5: 8, Luke 22: 41–42, Acts 7: 60, Acts 9: 40, 1 Timothy 2: 8, Psalm 28: 2, John 17: 1, Daniel 6: 10 and Luke 18: 11–13.

Prayer is open to everyone and can be enacted in family, groups or alone. The legendary literary figure from Daniel Defoe's novel, *Robinson Crusoe*, shipwrecked on a desert island and physically alone, cried out for the first time in prayer. He found joy, inner peace, forgiveness and comfort in his trials and burdens. Crusoe learned no-one need be an island — even when on one!

☐ *Doorway to purpose*
We affirm the discipline of fasting. Jesus at times fasted in order to attune spiritually. Fasting is found in all religious traditions of antiquity. It is good for our health — our digestive system has a break — and it enhances our spiritual growth. It gets us in touch with our own bodies; as meditator and onetime TM practitioner, Lynda Rose, says:

> *Positively, a fast can purify the system and so make us more spiritually receptive. Not all fasts, however, need necessarily involve renunciation of food. Some fasts, for example, might involve restriction on the amount of time spent in talking to people. I once decided that for twenty-four hours I would restrict what I said to only what was absolutely necessary. A word of warning here, however! Do tell people if you are going to do this, because otherwise they might assume that you are being rude.*[6]

☐ *Penetrating the cloud of unknowing*
We affirm the discipline of reflection on the Sacred Scriptures. Mysticism has rightly perceived that a full knowledge of God is beyond our own intuition. We have discovered that this cloud of unknowing is pierced through contemplation on the scriptures. This discipline will also lead us into an understanding of our own condition, knowledge of Jesus, detoxification of our inner impurities and the presence of the Spirit residing in our hearts.

Over the past few hundred years, many have become removed from any sense of devotional use of the Bible and have used it only for dogma. This approach has tended to isolate people of the heart (as against people of the head) from the Sacred Writings.

Relying on the perceptions of those like St Ignatius of Loyola, we recommend the following spiritual exercises when reading the Bible. It will bring wholeness, harmony and balance. It will also restore your dignity:

* **First**, find a quiet place where you can relax. Do not fold your legs; unfold your arms. Perhaps play some therapeutic music like Antonio Vivaldi's 'The Four Seasons'.
* **Second**, find a passage of scripture that is particularly open to attuning with. For example, the story of the women who encounter healing:

> *A ruler came and knelt before Jesus and said, 'My daughter has just died. But come and put your hand on her and she will live.' Jesus got up and went with him, and so did his disciples.*
>
> *Just then a woman who had been subject to bleeding for twelve years came up behind him and touched the edge of his cloak. She said to herself, 'If I only touch his cloak, I will be healed.'*
>
> *Jesus turned and saw her. 'Take heart,*

> *daughter,' he said, 'your faith has healed you.' And the woman was healed from that moment. When Jesus entered the ruler's house and saw the flute players and the noisy crowd, he said, 'Go away. The girl is not dead, but asleep.' But they laughed at him. After the crowd had been put outside, he went in and took the girl by the hand, and she got up.*[7]

* **Third**, become part of the scene by hearing the crowd, smelling the surroundings and seeing the characters.
* **Fourth**, become one of the characters (apart from Jesus) and live out their journey. As you do so, be in touch with how this touches your own emotions, hurts and joys.
* **Fifth**, let Jesus touch the character, touch you.

The power of scripture to bring one into an awareness of the divine and uphold one is seen in the film, 'The Elephant Man'. The film portrays a hideously grotesque and deformed being wearing a bag over his head. One day as he is walking, some hoodlums pull the bag off. He begins to run and people chase him, laughing and spitting.

More join the frenzied crowd. He runs into a toilet block and finds himself lying in the urinal. He cries out: 'I am not an animal; I am a human being!' The crowd falls silent and slinks away as they hear the Elephant Man's heartfelt cry of dignity.

Where did he find such understanding? Every night before he went to bed he used to say the 23rd

Psalm, 'The Lord is my shepherd. . . I will fear no evil, for you are with me.' This man knew from his reflections on the Sacred Writings that he was accepted by the Lord of the cosmos. There our self-esteem is renewed, too.

☐ *The awakening*
We affirm the discipline of meditation. Meditation is an ancient way of entering into a deep spiritual awareness of God. It is a pathway to rest, peace and the handling of stress, and to the energies of God (those times when we catch a glimpse of God and experience his presence).

Modern society is out of harmony with the environment. Our fast urban, concrete jungle lifestyles often disconnect us from the beauty of the natural world. As the Psalmist observed, there is great pleasure in our enjoyment of nature.[8] Meditation is an excellent tool which, if done outdoors, brings us an appreciation of our natural surroundings.

Lynda Rose has developed the following techniques for rewarding meditation:

* **First**, prepare yourself by finding a quiet spot and identifying your purpose for meditation.
* **Second**, choose one or more of the following God-given aids as your focus. This can be a passage of scripture, a word like 'peace' or 'Jesus' (*The Cloud of Unknowing* recommends all-embracing one-syllable words like *God*, *love*, *sin*), the Eastern Jesus Prayer ('Lord Jesus

Christ, Son of God, have mercy on me'), silence (that is, being still to allow God to talk to you — he leads the soul to pray), creation (seeing the handiwork of the Artist).

* **Third**, conclude your exercise. 'The ending of meditation should be the same. It should be relaxed and end with a brief prayer of thanks and dedication, and the eyes should only then be opened, slowly.'[9]

* **Fourth**, be prepared to face distractions such as pain, headaches and falling asleep. Acknowledge them, don't be deterred, gently refocus your attention on your exercise and, the more experienced you become, the less these things will occur.

❐ *Focussing*

We affirm the discipline of centring. Throughout the ages, those with spiritual insight have affirmed the importance of centring our life on a true master. It is the technique of detaching oneself from insignificant pursuits. In Olympic competition, athletes find they can zero in their thoughts to a single-minded focus on what lies before them.

Jesus stands before us as we see his humanity, divinity, purity, kindness, servanthood, love, death, resurrection and coming. As we concentrate on him, we are motivated to lead the authentic path of the fully conscious and wholly integrated person. It is also as we centre on Jesus that we receive the revelation that the coming 'New Age' is dependent on his in-breaking into the lives of us all.

Christian writer, Calvin Miller, draws us into the realm of Christ-focus:

Fellowship with Christ is a table only for two — set in the wilderness. Inwardness is not a gaudy party, but the meeting of lovers in the lonely desert of the human heart. There, where all life and fellowship can hold no more than two, we sit together and he speaks as much as we, and even when both of us say nothing there is our welded oneness. And suddenly we see we cannot be complete until his perfect presence joins with ours.[10]

❒ *Alchemy of the heart*
We affirm the discipline of spiritual breathing. When our lives are fixed on Jesus, the Spirit joins with us and fully immerses us in the sea of God. To reach the state of inner calm, all we have to do is breathe out our worries and ask the Holy Spirit to enter in. This is when our leaden ways are transformed into gold.[11]

❒ *Friends in high places*
We affirm the discipline of openness to angelic presence. One of the comforts of life is that we are surrounded by accompanying angels. Those who know this have tremendous peace and well-being. At times they even guide, as seen in the case of the first Christmas shepherds. They can bring answers to prayer.[12] In the story of Jesus, we learn that they bring strength to us in times of distress.[13]

Angels also protect us and the Psalmist implies that this may be done by our own special guardian angel.[14] Angels are particularly close to children[15] and convey us to the other side.[16] Sometimes, we may entertain angels unaware.[17]

The road to finding angels is the Sacred Scriptures. They declare that angels are created beings who serve God, whereas humans shall share in a greater glory than theirs.[18]

A friend of ours is Joan Eley, an Australian ministering in outback Venezuela. She recounts an exciting story. Travelling home on her motorbike late at night, she was informed that there was a group of men waiting to accost her. The attack didn't take place and in conversation the following day they were heard to say, 'Whom did Joan bring home with her?'

'No-one' was the reply. How was that possible — they saw someone dressed in white sitting on the pillion of her bike? As Joan testifies, who could that be 'but an angel of the Lord'! Such encounters are widely reported and it is exciting to see an upsurge of interest in angels at festivals and in print.[19]

Sadly, not all are aware of this angelic companionship. In the Sacred Writings, there is the story of the servant and the prophet Elisha. They were encompassed by enemy forces and the servant was lost in despair. Elisha prayed:

'O Lord, open his eyes so that he may see.' Then the Lord opened the servant's eyes, and he looked and saw the hills full of horses and chariots of fire all round Elisha.[20]

❏ *Opening the doorway to your true identity*
We affirm the discipline of imagination. Dreaming is a
tool that helps us contemplate our future and en-
visage personal growth and improvement. It is best
done by quietly assessing our gifts, talents and
desires and journaling where these could feasibly
take us. As the writer of Proverbs said, 'Where
there is no vision, the people get out of hand.'[21]
Imagination helps us set goals for life.

Cliff Jones writes:

> In the area of personal achievement, imagination frees
> us from breaking one of the Ten Commandments,
> 'Thou shalt not covet.' The temptation is to desire
> our neighbour's achievement rather than achieving
> ourselves. We can be fatally eaten up in the selfish
> pursuit of obtaining what belongs to another. The
> doorway to growth is to be found by releasing our-
> selves from this desire and by applying our own gifts
> and abilities to accomplish something uniquely ours.[22]

❏ *Whole person therapy*
We affirm the discipline of worship. Worship involves
the aspects of rest, music, interconnecting, praise
and everyday life. All are involved with worship,
be it self-worship or Divine worship.

Rest is an intrinsic part of Divine worship. It
is captured in the symbol of the sabbath. We
suggest rest is best exercised by taking time each
week to be inactive, sharing your time with Jesus,
family and friends. It brings physical release and

calm to the body, mind and spirit. Jesus, in the story of Mary and Martha, saw it as a therapeutic priority from which all else flows.

Martha, as a socially conscious Jewess, was busy preparing the meal, while Mary sat at the Master's feet. To Martha's critique of Mary's conduct, Jesus responded, 'Mary has chosen what is better and it will not be taken away from her.'[23]

Brother Jeremiah is earthy in his appreciation of rest:

If I had my life to live over, I would start barefooted earlier in the spring and stay that way later in the fall. I would play more. I would ride on more merry-go-rounds. I'd pick more daisies.[24]

Worship is not purely an isolated thing and it finds its best expression in a community. It is also about what we offer to the world, God and each other in our everyday life.

❑ *The tao of community*
We affirm the discipline of human togetherness. A major tool for recovery is community. In our era of mobilisation, the tendency is to live alone even though surrounded by a maze of apartments. Jesus called us to form a new community where there is support, encouragement and a sense of belonging.

Regrettably, within our communities there is today a superficial spirit. They have caught the

modern malaise of male distancing in relationships
and a lack of deep, honest communication. This
shallowness is not confined to churches and finds a
place in families, community groups and clubs.

The sensitive New Age guy, we believe, has had
enough of this:

> *Men have discovered a new kind of pain — loneliness
> and longing. For the first time, they are starting to
> hear from the boys inside themselves who were im-
> prisoned in suits of armour centuries ago and told to
> be men. They can no longer block out the need for
> intimacy, friendship, tenderness and creativity —
> those things dealing with 'being' rather than 'doing'.
> Having allowed the inner need to reach the surface,
> it is demanding to be heard.[25]*

One effective way of our allowing our communities to be strengthened is a form of
psychodrama. We suggest that the members
gather and take time to relax. Oneness is then
created by dividing into pairs and taking twelve
minutes to look into each other's eyes without
comment. This closeness will draw us to ask
meaningful questions of ourselves, like 'Why, as
a male, do I find it difficult to share in this
closeness?' and 'How long is it since I have just
been in the presence of my children?'

After this period of emotional intimacy, those
involved can take time to form a human sculpture
of how they felt — to choose someone to play their

part and indicate what stance they should take to represent themselves. For example, they can have palms open indicating they want to be accepted, or back turned showing a fear of closeness. Then other members in the group can be placed around the central 'player', representing how the 'director' believes his family and friends relate to him.

Into this drama, the Master Jesus can be asked to come to take our fears, to heal and to create what we truly desire.[26]

❑ *The power of the global vision*
We affirm the discipline of servanthood. As we have discussed, transformation is like a river that flows from our personal self to flood our global village with healing and recovery. The key to this is the tool of servanthood. Its dimension is the breaking down of the racial, social and sexual barriers that bind people to poverty in body, mind and spirit. It loathes starvation, deprivation, political oppression and ecological rape.

The discipline of servanthood begins in surrender of self to the Master Jesus who was the ultimate servant. Then one moves to concentrate again on him, not in the sense of personal growth, but for cosmic transformation. Jesus embraced the call of servanthood in the words, 'Greater love has no-one than this, that he lay down his life for his friends.'[27]

The essence of the personalised global servanthood path is in the prayer of St Francis of Assisi:

Lord, make me an instrument of your peace.
  Where there is hatred, let me sow love,
  Where there is injury, pardon,
  Where there is doubt, faith,
  Where there is despair, hope,
  Where there is darkness, light,
  Where there is sadness, joy.

O Divine Master, grant that I may not so much seek
  to be consoled as to console,
  not so much seek to be understood as
  to understand,
  not so much seek to be loved, as to love;
  for it is in giving that we receive,
  it is in pardoning that we are pardoned,
  it is in dying that we awake to eternal life.

❖ It's party time!

Those who find personal transformation in the above recovery tools will experience peace, strength, defeat of anxiety, inner satisfaction, friendship and purpose for life. Jesus sees his kingdom as a banquet celebration to which we are all invited. This party will ultimately engulf the world.[28]

As well as these gifts, there is real guidance for life. As one reflects on the Sacred Scriptures, prays, meditates, fasts and shares in community, *God* speaks. Sometimes his guidance is specific; at other times it is just knowing what is genuinely right. In the uniqueness of Jesus, individuals and nations can know and experience recovery.

The story comes from New Zealand of Helena

Pearson, who was looking for meaning in life. She was encouraged by friends to explore the spiritual paths available in India. She encountered Sai Baba, Swami Muktananda and Bhagwan Shree Rajneesh — all gurus that promised the sincere seeker enlightenment.

Helena Pearson describes how their self-driven, perfectionist quest impacted on her soul:

> *I'm so tired. I just want out. I want to go home and rest. I don't want your heaven any more, as I can't bear the hell that goes with it. I am not strong enough for your 'God'. Now I just want to be one of those ordinary people of the world that your gurus seem to despise so much.*

Her story concludes with her being left to reflect on the Sacred Writings and the techniques therein:

> *Helena clasped the fragile black book to her chest. Dare she risk walking into the labyrinth of Christianity? Would this new-found peace be a temporary phase of her life's journey? Or would it be deep and everlasting? There was only one way a person like Helena could find out.*[29]

❖ Insight: the horse and cart

In the last two hundred years, secularism has dominated the Western world. Some have seen it as two centuries of spiritual bankruptcy. In the post-Cold War world of modernity, the need for a spiritual dimension to life is being widely touted.

There is a need, then, for a new paradigm. Just as the horse and cart had to give way to the motor vehicle, secularism is being transcended. As Nevill Drury poignantly surmises: 'The cosmos awaits our arrival.'[30]

At the festival, the perennial discussion was over the form and shape of the new paradigm. There was common agreement that it would eventually involve a universal spirituality. It was also agreed that it would centre on some ancient spiritual practices. We explored many such practices with our friends: astrology, past-lives, channelling and divination. We found these to be anchored in self-guidance and created entities.

The tools we have stressed for the road to transformation stretch beyond the limitations of this realm and are centred in the Creator. These are the tools of prayer, fasting, reflection, meditation, imagination, focus, worship, community and global vision.

*   *   *

As we stand on the threshold of a New Age — an aquarian dream of unity — will the spiritual methods of the Lord Jesus be our quest? Will we experience him and allow him to be our guide and star?

> *Listen! I am standing at the door, knocking. If you hear my voice and open the door, I will come in to you and eat with you, and you with me.*[31]

The table is set. Let's join in the party!

Appendix 1:

Seeing the New Age connections

AS AN AID TO OUR UNDERSTANDING of the New Sense, we believe it is fruitful to list some of the influential sources and figures in the rise of the movement.

❖ Sources
The following chart we have found is a good introduction:

Ingredients for the New Age

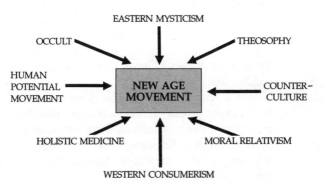

* *Eastern mysticism*:   Since the age of European colonial expansion, Western societies have increasingly come into direct and serious contact with the spiritual traditions of Asia (Hinduism, Jainism, Buddhism, Taoism, Shintoism).   Understandably, in a multi-cultural society, such traditions are even more evident.
* *Theosophy:*   The Theosophical Society established by Madame Blavatsky in 1875 became a funnel into which Eastern, Western and Occult traditions merged.   Madame Blavatsky channelled the Tibetan masters' teachings into the West.   Theosophy came to represent universal brotherhood, psychic realm and syncretism.
* *Counter-culture*: The late 1960s was an exciting period of political ferment where people experimented with alternative lifestyles, meditation, mind-altering drugs and gurus. In some sense, it was the genesis of the yuppie baby-boomers of today.
* *Occult*: Although there have long been various esoteric traditions around the world where such practices as astrology, palmistry, witchcraft and divination were found, many of these have enjoyed a popular revival since the advent of the counter-culture. Occult means the secret or hidden things.
* *Human potential movement*: The elements of this movement stem from various psychotherapeutic theories such as those propounded by Maslow and Erickson. The basic belief is attaining 'peak experiences' through the mind powers techniques.

Many seminars were developed in the 'Me-Decade' of the 1970s. Some of the prominent practitioners of these various principles are: Werner Erhard, Jose Silva, Wayne Dyer, John Kehoe, Roy Masters, Eric Jensen, Shakti Gawain and Jean Houston.

Celebrities who give testimony to the benefits of these teachers and their programs are: John Denver, Cher, Yoko Ono, Diana Ross, Kate Ceberano, Tom Cruise, Nicole Kidman, Patrick Swayze and former Sydney Lord Mayor, Jeremy Bingham.

* *Holistic health*: See chapter 5 for the details.
* *Western consumerism*: The commercial enterprises of the American scene where 'commodities' are sold have been translated into the contemporary religious scene. Religion is now like any other commercial 'product' which may be purchased in a large supermarket.
* *Moral relativism*: A major characteristic of our global village is the notion that truth is just a matter of personal preferences as summed up in the oft-used expression, 'That's your truth — I have my own.' Our world of human rights abuses, oppressive regimes and discriminatory work practices show the deficiency of leaving each authority, employer or person to their own ethic.

The great analytical philosopher and religious sceptic, Ludwig Wittgenstein, has suggested that ethics must be transcendental if they are to be of universal assistance.

❖ Influential figures

* *Emmanuel Swedenborg* (1688–1772) was a Swedish scientist who spent the last thirty years of his life pursuing spiritual experiences with angelic beings. Along with the development of psychic and clairvoyant powers, he reinterpreted the Bible as a 'parable' of the spiritual realm which has its exact correspondence in the physical world.

  Among his many books are *Arcana Coelestia* and *Heaven and Its Wonders and Hell*. After his death, the Church of the New Jerusalem was created by his followers and still exists today.

* *Mary Baker Eddy* (1821–1910) was the founder of Christian Science. In her book, *Science and Health with Key to the Scriptures*, she taught that the material world, evil, pain, sickness and death are an illusion. She said God was a principle in everything. Sickness and evil are overcome by recognising they are illusory. Her teachings influenced many other groups like New Thought, and Unity School of Christianity and Religious Science.

* *Swami Vivekananda* (1863–1902) was the first Hindu missionary to the West and founded the Vedanta Society. He addressed the World Parliament of Religions at Chicago in 1893. He taught that all is God (pantheism) and that we are therefore all divine.

* *Helena Blavatsky* (1831–1891) was the co-founder of the Theosophical Society, which is mentioned above.

* *Charles Leadbeater* (1854–1934) was the first bishop of the Liberal Catholic Church in Australia. He was closely associated with Theosophy and his ideas have had a tremendous impact on the New Age.

    Greg Tillett observes: 'The modern occult revival (global) owes more to him than to anyone else; his concepts and ideas, his popularising of occult and Theosophical terms and principles run through all modern works on these subjects. . . Words like *karma, chakra, chela, Mahatma, atma, Buddhi, manas, Maitreya. . .* have continued to be used in the sense in which he used them, regardless of their original meanings, by writers and theorists who give no acknowledgment to Leadbeater as the origin of their ideas.'[1]

* *Alice Bailey* (1880–1949) was the founder of the Arcane School and Lucis Trust. She was an early participant in Theosophy, but left to form her own movement. She was a prolific writer who claimed her teachings came from an ascended master, Djwhal Khul. She believed in the coming of the World Teacher, Lord Maitreya, who would usher in the New Age. She wrote the 'Great Invocation', a prayer frequently used by New Agers and occultists.

* *Rudolf Steiner* (1861–1925) was the founder of Anthroposophy, an offshoot from Theosophy. Steiner rejected the Eastern philosophical bent of Theosophy in favour of a mystical-occult interpretation of Christianity. He taught that

the earth had passed through seven epochs and that the Eastern religions merely prepared the way for Christ. He also taught reincarnation, herbalism and created the sacred dance form called *eurhythmy*.

His followers are well-known for using homeopathy. Homeopaths dilute healing substances to show the patient's need for maximum dependency on the element's Life Force. For example, in biodynamic farming, specially consecrated manure is diluted and sprayed over the crops. His influence extends into the Steiner schools for children's education and in the church gathered around his teachings, The Christian Community.

* *Nicholas Roerich* (1874–1947) was a Russian artist and mystic who founded the Agni Yogi Society. He was involved with Theosophy and the Arcane School, and translated some of Blavatsky's books into Russian. He believed that art could unify humanity. He travelled in Tibet and claimed to verify Notovitch's claims concerning Jesus' visit to India and Tibet.

Roerich's wife received messages from the entity Master Morya. These have been published in thirteen volumes and form the basis of agni yoga.

* *Edgar Cayce* (1877–1945) was a trance medium noted for the 'readings' he gave on illness, healing, reincarnation, psychic powers, Jesus in India, etc. His work is promoted today by the Association for Research and Enlightenment.

* *Arthur Ford* (1897–1971) was a prominent

spiritualist medium who founded the International General Association of Spiritualists. He believed in reincarnation and practised trance readings through a spirit guide named Fletcher. He rose to fame for revealing the secret code Harry Houdini gave to his wife before he died — a code Houdini was to give his wife as proof he survived beyond the grave. He also conducted a televised seance for the Episcopal Bishop James Pike when Pike's son committed suicide.

* *Alan Watts* (1915–1973) was an Episcopal priest who quit the church and became a Buddhist. His many books, such as *The Way of Zen, This Is It, Beat Zen, Square Zen and Zen*, had a major impact on the counter-culture of the 1960s.

* *Wilhelm Reich* (1897–1957) was the pioneer of 'bodywork' therapy. This entails an energy called *orgone* flowing through the body and is supposed to be the basis of love and orgasm. Painful traumas block the flow of energy, giving rise to physical and mental illness.

    These blocks, called 'body armour', were broken by techniques Reich developed to release one's physical, sexual and emotional energy. Breathing exercises, massage, convulsive reflex work, kicking and stamping release the energy. His ideas have influenced New Age therapies like bioenergetics, Rolfing, Feldenkrais, polarity therapy and biodynamic massage.

* *Paul Twitchell* (1908?–1971) was the founder of

Eckankar which promotes the art of soul-travel, hearing the Divine Cosmic Sound, and interpreting dreams and inner consciousness.

One of Twitchell's former disciples is John-Roger Hinkins, the founder of Insight Transformational Seminars and the Church of the Movement of Spiritual Inner Awareness (MSIA).

* *Walter Burley Griffin (1876–1937)* was the US architect who designed the Australian capital city of Canberra. Griffin was powerfully influenced by Swedenborg and joined Theosophy. With his wife, Marion, he endeavoured to design the ideal city based on the principles of 'sacred geometry', geomancy and *feng shui*. The location of the Federal Parliament House, city gardens and circular roads were intended to radiate cosmic harmony with the nearby mountains. The revival of geomancy and *feng shui* in architectural designs for buildings can be seen in many European, American and Australasian cities.[2]

Appendix 2:

Learning from each other

ONE OF THE ILLUMINES OF HISTORY that we admire the most is Hugo Grotius. He was the seventeenth century maverick, ambassador, philosopher and founder of our modern international law. He awakened the world to this principle:

> *For my part, both here and elsewhere, I avail myself of the liberty of the early Christians, who had sworn allegiance to the sect of no one of the philosophers, not because they were in agreement with those who said that nothing can be known — nothing is more foolish — but because they thought that there was no philosophic sect whose vision had encompassed all truth, and none which had not perceived some aspect of truth.*[1]

In this spirit, we desire to probe what forgotten truths the New Age and Christian devotees can learn from each other.

❖ Forgotten truths for New Agers

* *Diversity:* Diversity is a fact of life. Some New Agers portray the movement as a harmonious whole without the conflict of ideas. And whilst there is a real warmth felt at New Age gatherings that creates a sense of oneness, it is by no means the whole story. As you walk around festivals, you discover groups with contradictory approaches to life and differing emphases, often competing with each other for disciples.

  One illustration of this 'conflict' is Reiki. There are a number of groups, each claiming connections with the same authoritative spiritual master and yet each denying the authenticity of their rivals. It is time for the New Age to accept that, like the world, all is not one in spirit.

* *Tolerance:* New Agers often speak of Christians being intolerant of other paths due to their exclusive emphasis on Jesus Christ as the only way to God. The forgotten truth, though, is that philosophically tolerance doesn't demand acceptance of other views; rather, its focus is on the right of people to hold them. It is summed up in this aphorism: 'I may disagree with your view, but I'll defend your right to hold it.' *That's* tolerance! And it is intolerant to impose universalism on others.

* *Truth:* On the whole, the New Age movement avoids the truth question. It simply claims that the truth is found in all paths. Marianne Williamson decrees: 'Religion is like a map. The

route isn't important. It's the destination that matters.'[2] The difficulty is that this in itself is an assertion which has not been proven. As well, we have identified that Jesus' teaching on life after death substantially differs from the New Age. The New Sense 'plane' is not going to the same destination.

Another concern with this approach to religious endeavour is that it's disrespectful to the integrity of the basic claims of each major tradition. For example for Muslims, Islam is the only true path to God.

Mortimer Adler, considered to be America's philosopher for the layperson, stated that the truth question in religion cannot be avoided or trivialised. Adler has issued this clarion call:

I would like to hear leading twentieth-century theologians speaking as apologists for Judaism, Christianity and Islam [dare we add New Age?] engage in a disputation. The question at issue would be which of these three religions had a greater claim to truth. It being conceded that each has a claim to some measure of truth, which of the three can rightly claim more truth than the other two?[3]

Philosopher Francis Beckwith has this poetic, gentle rebuke:

    'All roads lead to God,'
    I've heard so many people say,

> *But when they get to Jonestown*
> *They beg to look the other way.*[4]

The New Age still has to face Pilate's appeal to Jesus, 'What is truth?'

❖ Forgotten truths for Christians

* *Enjoying God:* One of the Christian creeds states that our chief end is to glorify God and enjoy him forever. The New Age has perceived that the second part of the creed has been lost in parts of modern-day Christianity. Dry orthodoxy, dogma and irrelevant liturgy must never replace the joyful experience of the Spirit.

* *Nine-to-five spirituality:* Contemporary Christianity in some domains has lost the understanding of vocation. Ministry is seen as what is done for the church. New Age in contrast has re-emphasised through many of its seminars the importance of people being encouraged and equipped for living in the workforce and at home. It seeks to make better salespersons.

  The 'Sunday' spirituality of contemporary Christendom is not part of its inheritance. The apostle Paul had a theology of everyday life where he talked about foods to eat, relationships and the workforce, sexuality and the world of nine-to-five. However, the path back to authentic spirituality is being addressed by contemporary theologians like Robert Banks and must become part of the church's teaching ministry if New Agers are to find the Christian faith relevant.[5]

Another area of concern is that of guidance. Christians struggle in today's age to know the will of God. In contrast, those like clairvoyants offer quick solutions. There is a real need for a practical theology of guidance. In Chapter 10, we stressed how guidance can be found when one relies on the tools of recovery.

* *Creation-centred spirituality:* Western Christianity has drifted into a humanised spirituality that is divorced from the rest of creation. It has compartmentalised faith by separating it from everything else. This is not good enough. Biblical justice is concerned about the liberation of all of creation — the trees, the dolphins and the refugee.[6] Personal meditation is enhanced by reflection upon the beauty of creation.[7]

The challenge is to hear again the words of Teilhard de Chardin: 'Nothing here below is profane for those who know how to see. On the contrary, everything is sacred.'[8]

* *The 'Hume' attack:* Christians tend to reduce the miraculous phenomena of other paths to natural explanations or fraudulent behaviour. Have Christians forgotten that the eighteenth century philosopher David Hume did the same to them? He suggested that at all times one should seek a natural explanation rather than accept the miracle stories of the Bible.

The truth or otherwise of miraculous occurrences does not rest on our hostility towards a group. All miraculous phenomena need to be tested and not simply be dismissed.

* *The missionary model:* In today's global village,

Christians need to remember Paul's missionary model to become 'all things to all people' (1 Corinthians 9: 16-22). As Christians now live side by side with Buddhists, Hindus, Muslims and New Agers, older techniques for sharing must give way to a missions model which is not only biblical, but also relevant to living in postmodernity. In Acts 17, Paul shared his faith in the synagogue with Jewish people who shared the Hebrew scriptures and culture. He dialogued with them about Jesus being the Messiah foretold in their scriptures.

However, when Paul dialogued with the Greeks in Athens, he entered their world view. He sought some common ground with the Greek philosophers as an entry point to sharing the good news. Paul chose to quote the Stoic philosophers as his entry point and so demonstrated that he understood their world view. He went on to speak about Jesus, the resurrection and judgment which was consistent with his preaching everywhere else. That day, some people came to faith (Acts 17:34).

Sadly, some Christians think that Paul was a failure in Athens. Such a view is inconsistent with the text. Moreover, leading scholars such as F.F. Bruce, E.M. Blaiklock, Alister McGrath, John Warwick Montgomery and Ned Stonehouse all agree that Acts 17 is a handsome illustration of the mission model we should all be using today.

* *Growing together:* Christian scholar Dr John Drane rightly suggests that New Age is saying something to the church about its togetherness:

The church should be a place where we can be accepted as we are — children, women and men together — a safe environment in which to discover more about ourselves, to experience personal growth and to make a contribution to the growth of others. When so very few of our congregations even begin to approximate to that ideal, need we be surprised that honest people look elsewhere?[9]

The church should continue to develop healing communities and strive against becoming cold, bureaucratic and ecclesiastical ghettoes. Let the Spirit of Christ reign.

❖ Insight

It would be a narrow position that held that the church has nothing to learn from the New Age or the New Age from the teachings of Christ. Throughout these pages, we have suggested that Christians need to hear the plea for a workable spirituality and New Agers the cry of the unique-ness of Jesus Christ.

For those involved in the spiritual journey, we leave you with these words of well-known writer, James Sire. They are addressed to Christians but, human nature being what it is, they apply to all:

A siege mentality is at work. Those who hold cultic ideas are seen as the enemy, the great threat to humanity, to Christian — even, some seem to suggest, to God himself. . . So in response anything goes: innuendo, name-calling, backhanded remarks, assumption of the worst motives on the part of the cult believers. And thus the Christian dehumanises the enemy and shoots him like a dog. But the Christian in this process is himself dehumanised.[10]

Appendix 3:

Selected reading list

I. Astrology and psycho-technologies

Eileen Campbell & J.H. Brennan, *The Aquarian Guide to the New Age*, Aquarian Press, 1990

Russell Chandler, *Understanding the New Age*, Word, 1988

Alfred Douglas, *The Tarot*, Penguin, 1973

Nevill Drury, *Healers, Quacks or Mystics?*, Hale & Iremonger, 1983

Nevill Drury, *The Shaman and the Magician*, Arkana, 1987

Cherry Gilchrist, *The Elements of Alchemy*, Element Books, 1991

Healers on Healing, Richard Carlson & Benjamin Shield (eds), Rider, 1990

Janis Huntley, *The Elements of Astrology*, Element Books, 1990

Judy Jacka, *Meditation: The Most Natural Therapy*, Lothian, 1990

Fiona McCallum, *Dear Fiona*, Pan, 1991

Elliot Miller, *A Crash Course on the New Age Movement*, Baker, 1989

John Warwick Montgomery, *Principalities and Powers*, Bethany House, 1973

Jonn Mumford, *Ecstasy Through Tantra*, Llewellyn Publications, 1988

The New Age Catalogue, Doubleday, 1988

Don Richard Riso, *The Practical Guide to Personality Types: Understanding the Enneagram*, Aquarian Press, 1991

Ramtha: An Introduction, Steven Lee Weinberg (ed.), Sovereignty Inc., 1988

II. Life after death, reincarnation and myth

Joseph Campbell with Bill Moyers, *The Power of Myth*, Doubleday, 1988

David Christie-Murray, *Reincarnation: Ancient Beliefs and Modern Evidence*, Dorset, 1988

Bruce Elder, *And When I Die, Will I Be Dead?*, Australian Broadcasting Corporation, 1987

Mircea Eliade, *Myths, Dreams and Mysteries*, Harper, 1975

Gary R. Habermas & J.P. Moreland, *Immortality: The Other Side of Death*, Thomas Nelson, 1992

Irving Hexham & Karla Poewe, *Understanding Cults and New Religions*, Eerdmans, 1986

Noel Langley, *Edgar Cayce on Reincarnation*, Warner, 1967

C.S. Lewis, *The Chronicles of Narnia*, Collier, 1970

Raymond Moody, *Life After Life*, Bantam, 1976

Maurice Rawlings, *Beyond Death's Door*, Bantam, 1979

Maurice Rawlings, *To Hell and Back*, Thomas Nelson, 1993

Jeffrey B. Russell, *The Prince of Darkness: Radical Evil and the Power of Good in History*, Thames & Hudson, 1989

Cherie Sutherland, *Transformed by the Light: Life after Near-Death Experiences*, Bantam, 1992

J.R.R. Tolkien, *The Lord of the Rings*, George Allen & Unwin, 1974

Ian Wilson, *The After Death Experience*, Corgi, 1989

Carol Zaleski, *Otherworld Journeys*, Oxford University Press, 1987

III. Christ consciousness, cosmic oneness, ecology and mind powers

Patricia Aburdene & John Naisbitt, *Megatrends for Women*, Villard, 1992

Per Beskow, *Strange Tales about Jesus*, Fortress, 1983

Janet Bock, *The Jesus Mystery*, Aura, 1980

Ian Bradley, *God is Green*, Doubleday, 1990

Fritjof Capra, *The Tao of Physics*, 3rd ed., Flamingo, 1991

Fritjof Capra and David Steindl-Rast with Thomas Matus, *Belonging to the Universe: New Thinking about God and Nature*, Penguin, 1992

Ross Clifford, *The Case for the Empty Tomb*, Albatross/Lion, 1993

Teilhard de Chardin, *The Future of Man*, Fontana, 1969

Sydney L. Donahoe, *Earth Keeping: Making It a Family Habit*, Zondervan, 1990

Nevill Drury, *The Visionary Human: Mystical Consciousness & Paranormal Perspectives*, Bantam, 1991

Wayne Dyer, *Real Magic: Creating Miracles in Everyday Life*, Harper Collins, 1992

Marilyn Ferguson, *The Aquarian Conspiracy: Personal and Social Transformation in the 1980s*, Paladin, 1982

Matthew Fox, *The Coming of the Cosmic Christ*, Collins Dove, 1988

Shakti Gawain, *Return to the Garden*, New World Library, 1989

Bede Griffiths, *A New Vision of Reality*, Fount Paperbacks, 1992

Douglas Groothuis, *Confronting the New Age*, InterVarsity Press, 1988

Dawn Hill, *With a Little Help from My Friends*, Pan, 1991

Eric Jensen, *Superteaching*, Turning Point, 1988

John Kehoe, *Mind Power*, Zoetic Inc., 1987

Ken Keyes, *Handbook to Higher Consciousness*, 5th edition, Love Line, 1975

Shirley MacLaine, *Going Within*, Bantam, 1989

Sandy MacGregor, *Piece of Mind*, CALM, 1992

George A. Malone, *Mysticism and the New Age: Christ Consciousness in the New Creation*, Albar House, 1991

Vishal Mangalwadi, *In Search of Self: Beyond the New Age*, Hodder, 1992

Art and Jocele Meyer, *Earth Keepers*, Herald Press, 1991

John Naisbitt & Patricia Aburdene, *Megatrends 2000*, Pan, 1990

John Polkinghorne, *One World: The Interaction of Science and Theology*, SPCK, 1986

Elizabeth Clare Prophet, *The Lost Years of Jesus*, Summit University Press, 1984

Ron Rhodes, *The Counterfeit Christ of the New Age Movement*, Baker, 1990

Paul Solomon, *The Meta-Human*, Hampton Roads, 1985

Charlene Spretnak, *States of Grace*, Harper, 1991

Transpersonal Psychologies, Charles Tart (ed.), Harper & Row, 1975

Marianne Williamson, *A Return to Love*, Aquarian Press, 1992

Morag Zwartz, *The New Age Gospel: Christ or Counterfeit?*, Parenesis, 1987

IV. Recovery

Karen Armstrong, *The English Mystics of the Fourteenth Century*, Kyle Cathie, 1991

Breakthrough: Meister Eckhart's Creation, Matthew Fox (ed.), Image, 1977

* Sheila Cassidy, *Prayer For Pilgrims*, Fount Paperbacks, 1980

The Cloud of Unknowing, Clifton Walters (trans.), Penguin, 1961

Terry Colling, *Beyond Mateship*, Simon & Schuster, 1992

Creation Spirituality & the Dreamtime, Catherine Hammond
(ed.), Millennium, 1991
* Richard Foster, *Prayer: Finding the Heart's True Home*,
Harper, 1992
* *High Mountains, Deep Valleys*, Rowland Croucher &
Grace Thomlinson (eds), Albatross/Lion, 1991
* Bill Hybels, *Who You Are When No One's Looking*, Inter-
Varsity Press, 1984
* Calvin Miller, *The Table of Inwardness*, InterVarsity Press,
1984
* M. Scott Peck, *Further Along the Road Less Travelled*,
Simon and Schuster, 1993
* Lynda Rose, *No Other Gods*, Hodder & Stoughton, 1990
M. Scott Peck, *Further Along The Road Less Travelled*, Simon
& Schuster, 1993
* R.C. Sproul, *The Hunger For Significance*, Regal, 1991
* Peter Toon, *What Is Spirituality and Is It For Me?*,
Daybreak, 1989

V. Personal journeys
Randall Baer, *Inside the New Age Nightmare*, Huntington
House, 1989
Tal Brooke, *Lord of The Air*, Harvest House, 1990
Tal Brooke, *Riders of the Cosmic Circuit*, Lion/Albatross,
1986
Mary Garden, *The Serpent Rising: A Journey of Spiritual
Seduction*, Brolga, 1988
Rabindranath Maharaj with Dave Hunt, *Death of A Guru*,
Hodder & Stoughton, 1977

VI. Appendices
Mortimer Adler, *Truth in Religion: The Plurality of Religions
and the Unity of Truth*, Collier, 1990

David Clark, *Dialogical Apologetics*, Baker, 1993

John Drane, *Evangelism for a New Age*, Marshall Pickering, 1994

John Drane, *What is the New Age Saying to the Church?*, Marshall Pickering, 1991

Jessica Lipnack and Jeffrey Stamps, *The Networking Book*, Routledge & Kegan Paul, 1986

Alistair McGrath, *Bridge Building*, InterVarsity Press, 1992

J. Gordon Melton, *New Age Almanac*, Visible Ink Press, 1991

David Millikan and Nevill Drury, *Worlds Apart? Christianity & the New Age*, Australian Broadcasting Corporation, 1991

Harold Netland, *Dissonant Voices: Religious Pluralism and the Question of Truth*, Eerdmans/Apollos, 1991

David Spangler and William Irwin Thompson, *Reimagination of the World*, Bear, 1991

Rachel Storm, *In Search of Heaven on Earth*, Aquarian Press, 1992

Charles Strohmer, *Wise as a Serpent, Harmelss as a Dove*, Nelson Word, 1994

Rachel Storm, *In Search of Heaven on Earth*, Aquarian Press, 1992

Charles Strohmer, *Wise as a Serpent, Harmless as a Dove*, Nelson Word, 1994

Explanatory note:
* Signifies those books which the authors have personally found to be very helpful in the road to recovery.

Endnotes

Chapter 1

1. Cherie Sutherland, *Transformed by the Light*, Bantam, 1992, p.10
2. David Spangler, *The New Age Catalogue*, Doubleday, 1988
3. John 14: 2
4. *Simply Living*, Vol.2, No.7
5. Bruce Elder, *And When I Die, will I be Dead?*, Australian Broadcasting Corporation, 1987
6. *The Aquarian Guide to the New Age*, Aquarian Press, 1990, p.224
7. Carol Zaleski, *Otherworld Journeys*, OUP, 1987, p.3
8. Elizabeth Taylor, in *Australian Women's Weekly*, June 1992, p.8
9. 'What I Saw When I Was Dead', in Terry Miethe and Antony Flew, *Does God Exist?*, Harper Collins, 1991, p.228
10. *Immortality: The Other Side of Death*, Thomas Nelson, 1992, p.104
11. See Ian Wilson, *The After Death Experience*, Corgi, 1989, pp.164–200.
12. Carol Zaleski, *op.cit*, p.190
13. James Mauro, 'Bright Lights, Big Mystery,' *Psychology Today*, July/August 1992, p.57

14. 'Eternity Now', *Simply Living*, Vol.6, No.5, p.60

15. Cherie Sutherland, *op.cit.*, p.18

16. *Closer to the Light: Learning from the Near-Death Experiences of Children*, Bantam, 1992, p.226

17. Robert Monroe, in Nevill Drury, *The Visionary Human*, Bantam, 1991, p.130

18. Maurice Rawlings, *Beyond Death's Door*, Bantam, 1979, pp xii-xiii. See also his sequel *To Hell And Back*, Thomas Nelson, 1993.

19. 'Deathbed Observations by Physicians and Nurses', in *Journal of the American Society for Psychical Research*, July 1977, p.30

20. Raymond Moody, Foreword to George Ritchie with Elizabeth Sherrill, *Return from Tomorrow*, Kingsway, 1978, p.9

21. Maurice Rawlings, *op.cit.*, p.46

22. Cherie Sutherland, *Within the Light*, Bantam, 1993, p.141

23. George Gallup Jr with William Proctor, *Adventures in Immortality*, Souvenir Press, 1983, p.73-87

24. Tom Harpur, *Life After Death*, McClelland & Stewart, 1992, p.51

25. Maurice Rawlings, *To Hell and Back*, Thomas Nelson, 1993

26. Margot Grey, *Return from Death*, Arkana, 1985

27. A paraphrase of Luke 16:19-31

Chapter 2

1. J. Head & S. Cranston, *Reincarnation: The Phoenix Fire Mystery*, Theosophical University Press, 1977, p.145

2. Malachi 4: 5

3. Matthew 11: 14

4. Noel Langley, *Edgar Cayce on Reincarnation*, Warner, 1967, p.173

5. 2 Kings 2: 11–12

6. John 1: 21

7. Luke 1: 17

8. John 3: 3

9. John 11: 21–25; Luke 24: 36–47; Acts 2: 24 and 32; 1

Corinthians 15

10. Hebrews 9: 27

11. Caroline Bing, 'Di's Astrologer Looks Ahead,' *The Australian Women's Weekly*, September 1992, p.12

12. Philippians 3: 20–21

13. *On First Principles*, Book 2, chs 6–9

14. Commentary on the Gospel of Matthew, Book 13, chapter 1

15. *Dialogue With Trypho*, chapter 4

16. See Dr Paul Badham, 'Recent Thinking on Christian Beliefs', *The Expository Times*, Vol.88, April 1977, pp.197–201.

17. John 9: 1–3

18. Galatians 6: 7 (NRSV)

19. Romans 8: 28

20. Lord Hailsham, *The Door Wherein I Went*, Collins, 1975, pp.40–41

21. Ian Stevenson, *Twenty Cases Suggestive of Reincarnation*, University of Virginia Press, 1966, pp.48, 228-229, 340-347

22. Elizabeth Stark, citing psychologists Bowers and Dywan (writing in *Science* magazine) in 'Hypnosis on Trial', *Psychology Today*, February 1984, p. 35

23. Elizabeth Loftus & Katherine Ketcham, *The Myth of Repressed Memory*, St Martin's Press, 1994; Richard Ofshe & Ethan Watters, *Making Monsters*, Charles Scribner's Sons, 1994; Hollida Wakefield & Ralph Underwager, *Return of the Furies*, Open Court, 1994

24. *Dictionary of Mysticism and the Occult*, Harper & Row, 1985, p.185

25. Stan Katz and Aimee Kiu, *The Codependency Conspiracy*, Warner, 1992, p.106

26. Philippians 3: 13

Chapter 3

1. Emile Grillot De Givry, *Illustrated Anthology of Witchcraft, Magic & Alchemy*, Dover, 1971, pp. 221, 226

2. Barry Eaton, 'Struck by the Stars,' *Bulletin*, 29 September 1992, p. 45

3. 'Scripture, Tradition and History in the Infancy Narratives of Matthew', in R.T. France & D. Wenham (eds), *Gospel Perspectives*, Vol.2, JSOT Press, 1981, p.257

4. Daniel 2: 27–28

5. Daniel 2: 48

6. Numbers 24: 15–17

7. The Histories, Book 5, 13

8. Daniel 9

9. Matthew 2: 10–11

10. Genesis 1: 14

11. Psalm 19: 1

12. Job 38: 31–33

13. Isaiah 47: 12–14

14. *Principalities and Powers*, Bethany, 1973, p.65

15. Kepler, *Harmony of the World*, in John Warwick Montgomery, *In Defense of Martin Luther*, Northwestern Publishing House, 1970, p.99

16. *Christianopolis*, chapter lxviii, as cited in John Warwick Montgomery, *Cross & Crucible*, Vol.1, Martinus Nijhoff, 1973, p.200

17. Psalm 19: 1–4 in the light of Romans 10: 17–18

18. In *Principalities and Powers*, op.cit., p.114

19. *The Scientific Basis of Astrology: Myth or Reality*, Stein & Day, 1973, p.145

20. Astrological Monthly Review, March 1992

21. *What Your Horoscope Doesn't Tell You*, Tyndale, 1988, pp.11, 109

22. Matthew 11: 28–29

Chapter 4

1. John Roger, *The Power Within You*, Baraka, 1976, p.1

2. Paul Solomon, *The Meta-Human: A Handbook for Personal Transformation*, Hampton Roads, 1985, p.9

3.. Dawn Hill, *With a Little Help from My Friends*, Pan, 1991, p.42

4. John 10: 30

5. *A Return to Love*, Aquarian Press, 1992, p.29
6. Psalm 8: 4–5 and 9 (NRSV)
7. Yasha 45: 2
8. Luke 4: 8
9. Acts 14: 15
10. Luke 17: 21
11. Acts 2
12. Matthew 28: 17
13. Galatians 3: 28
14. 'Away with the Pixies', *HQ Magazine*, Winter 1992, p.80
15. For discussion see Ian Bradley, *God is Green*, Doubleday, 1990, p.89
16. *The English Mystics of the Fourteenth Century*, Kyle Cathie, 1991, p.4
17. *Riders of the Cosmic Circuit*, Lion/Albatross, 1986, p.170. A fuller account of his journey is found in *Lord of the Air*, Harvest House, 1990
18. See *The Tao of Physics*. Flamingo, 1991
19. See *Belonging to the Universe*, Penguin, 1992
20. See Charles Birch, *On Purpose*, New South Wales University Press, 1990
21. See Darryl Reanney, *The Death of Forever*, Longman Cheshire, 1991
22. See Bryan Appleyard, *Understanding The Present: Science and the Soul of Modern Man*, Pan, 1992.
23. Hebrews 13: 5

Chapter 5

1. Geoffrey Keyte, Crystal Research Foundation, in *New Idea*, 8 September 1990, p.27
2. Louise Hay, *You Can Heal Your Life*, Specialist Publications, 1988, p.5
3. *Principalities and Powers, op. cit.*, pp.39–40
4. Matthew 17
5. 1 Samuel 28
6. 1 John 4: 1–3

7. Deuteronomy 18: 10–11

8. Randall Baer, *Inside The New Age Nightmare*, Huntington House, 1989, p.37

9. *Ibid*, p.38

10. See Mitchell Pacwa, 'Tell Me Who I Am, O Enneagram', *Christian Research Journal*, Vol.14/2, Fall 1991, pp.14–19 and also his book, *Catholics and the New Age*, Servant, 1992, pp.95-109

11. See Deuteronomy 13.

12. Jonathan Margolis, 'Are We Alone?', *Time Australia*, 31 August 1992, p.56

13. Matthew 24: 24

14. 1 John 4: 1–3

15. Samuel Pfeifer, *Healing at Any Price?*, Word Books, 1988

Chapter 6

1. Alan Lowen in Sharon Provost, 'The Tantric Way to Intimacy and Love', *Conscious Living*, No.11, February–March 1992, p.12

2. *Southern Crossings*, March/April 1992, p.21

3. *Sound Medicine*, pp.144–145

4. *The University of Sydney News*, October 16, 1984, p.255

5. *Megatrends for Women*, Villard, 1992, p.245

6. Romans 10: 13

7. Matthew 6: 8

8. Song of Songs, 8: 5–6, 10 and 14

9. 1 Samuel 16: 23

10. Ephesians 5: 19

11. See A.E. Waite, *The Pictorial Key to the Tarot*, US Games Systems, 1990, p.157; and John Warwick Montgomery, *Principalities and Powers*, Bethany, pp.129–131

12. Deuteronomy 18: 10–11

13. 'Deaths Followed Fortune-Teller Visits', *Sydney Morning Herald*, 25 July 1992, p.3

14. Randall Baer, *Inside the New Age Nightmare*, Huntington House, 1989, pp. 59 and 180

Chapter 7

1. Mircea Eliade, 'The Yearning for Paradise in Primitive Tradition,' in *Myth and Mythmaking*, Henry Murray (ed.), George Braziller, 1960, p.73
2. Joseph Campbell with Bill Moyers, *The Power of Myth*, Doubleday, 1988, p.10
3. *Ibid*, p.39
4. See *Myths, Dreams and Mysteries*, Harper, 1975, pp.43-47
5. Acts 17: 26, CEV
6. *The Prince of Darkness: Radical Evil and the Power of Good in History*, Thames & Hudson, 1989, pp.276–277
7. Colossians 1: 13
8. See 'The Evidence For Atlantis', *Christian Research Journal*, Vol.12/1 Summer 1989 pp.16–19.
9. Alvin Toffler, *Future Shock*, Random House, 1970, p.100
10. John Naisbitt, *Megatrends*, Warner, 1982, p.2
11. Luke 15: 14–32
12. 'On Fairy-Stories', in *Essays Presented To Charles Williams*, C.S. Lewis (ed), Eerdmans, 1981, pp.83-84
13. *The Aquarian Guide to the New Age*, p.38
14. Revelation 21: 1–4, NRSV

Chapter 8

1. John Kehoe, *Mind Power*, Zoetic, 1987, p.23
2. Shirley MacLaine, *Going Within*, Bantam, 1989, pp.46,47
3. Mark 9: 23
4. *The New Age Catalogue*, Doubleday, 1988, p.85
5. Charles Paul Brown, Bernadeane and James Russell Strole, *Together Forever*, Pythagorean Press, 1991, p.72
6. 'Dark Side of The New Age', *The Weekend Australian*, 13–14 January 1990
7. For a discussion of these points, refer to Douglas Groothuis, *Confronting the New Age*, InterVarsity Press, 1988, pp.163–165
8. Luke 10: 29–37
9. Proverbs 23: 7

10. Jeremiah 1: 5
11. Luke 10: 36–37
12. Matthew 5: 25
13. Mark 6: 31
14. 1 Corinthians 1 and 2
15. Matthew 5: 26
16. Philippians 4: 6–7
17. *The New Age Catalogue*, op.cit., p.157
18. Ric Chapman and Ross Clifford, *The Gods of Sport*, Albatross/Lion, 1995

Chapter 9

1. Janet Bock, *The Jesus Mystery*, Aura, 1980, p.5
2. A.K.Tebecis, *Mahikari: Thank God for the Answers at Last*, Yoko Shuppansha, 1982, p.358
3. Matthew 2: 13
4. See *The Aquarian Gospel of Jesus the Christ*, Fowler, 1964
5. See C.C. Dobson, *Did Our Lord Visit Britain as They Say in Cornwall and Somerset?*, Covenant, 1974
6. *The Life of St Issa*, 5: 1–2
7. October 1894, pp. 515–521
8. 'The Chief Lama of Himis on the Alleged "Unknown Life of Christ"', *The Nineteenth Century*, April 1896, pp.671–672, 677
9. Christmas Humphreys, *Buddhism*, Penguin, 1962, pp.190–191
10. Paul Pappas, *Jesus' Tomb in India*, Asian Humanities Press, 1991, p.154
11. Enakshi Bhavnani, 'A Journey to "Little Tibet"', *National Geographic*, Vol.99, 1951, p.624
12. The Gospel of Thomas, saying 114
13. The Essene Gospel of Peace, Vol.1, pp.22–23
14. *Strange Tales About Jesus*, Fortress, 1983, p.88
15. Richard France, *The Evidence for Jesus*, Hodder, 1985, p.14
16. Luke 1: 1–4
17. John 10: 8–9, John 14: 6; John 11: 25; Mark 10: 45
18. Psalm 148: 1–4; Psalm 8; Hebrews 2; 1 Corinthians 6: 3; and Romans 8: 16–17

19. Meister Eckhart, Sermon 53
20. Ecclesiastes 2: 24
21. Romans 2
22. A *Course in Miracles*, Text, Arkana, 1985, p.88
23. A *Course in Miracles*, Workbook, Arkana, 1985, p.172
24. *A Course in Miracles*, Text, Arkana, 1985, p.223
25. SCP Journal, Vol.7, No.1, 1987, p.32

Chapter 10

1. Robert Fulghum, *All I Really Need to Know I Learned in Kindergarten*, Grafton Books/Collins, 1989, p.6
2. Matthew Fox, in *Creation Spirituality and the Dreamtime*, Catherine Hammond (ed.), Millennium, 1991, p.4
3. Luke 18: 17
4. *Ibid*
5. R.A. Torrey, *The Power of Prayer*, Zondervan, 1972, p.190
6. Lynda Rose, *No Other Gods*, Hodder, 1990, pp.138–139
7. Matthew 9: 18–25. Other suitable passages include the Book of Ruth, Gospel miracle stories, 2 Kings 4–6, the Book of Exodus
8. Psalm 16: 11
9. Lynda Rose, *No Other Gods*, Hodder, 1990, p.155
10. Calvin Miller, *The Table of Inwardness*, InterVarsity Press, 1984, p.22
11. Galatians 5: 16–23
12. Daniel 10: 11–21
13. Luke 22: 43
14. Psalm 91: 11–12
15. Matthew 18: 10
16. Luke 16: 22
17. Hebrews 13: 2
18. Psalm 148: 1–4; Psalm 8; Hebrews 2; 1 Corinthians 6: 3; and Romans 8: 16–17
19. Joan Eley, *God's Brumby*, p.187
20. 2 Kings 6: 17
21. Proverbs 29: 18, Jerusalem Bible

22. Cliff Jones, *Winning Through Integrity*

23. Luke 10: 38–42

24. Brother Jeremiah, in Ted Engstrom, *The Pursuit of Excellence*, p.90

25. Terry Colling, *Beyond Mateship*, Simon & Schuster, 1992, p.x

26. For further helpful explorations on community, see M.Scott Peck, *The Different Drum*, Arrow Books, 1990

27. John 15: 13

28. John 14: 27, Philippians 4: 13, 1 Peter 2: 7, Hebrews 13: 5, John 14: 6, Matthew 6: 10

29. Mary Garden, *The Serpent Rising*, Brolga Publishing, 1988, pp.172 and 180

30. Nevill Drury, *The Visionary Human*, p.123

31. Revelation 3: 17, NRSV

Appendix 1

1. Greg Tillett, *The Elder Brother: A Biography of Charles Webster Leadbeater*, Routledge & Kegan Paul, 1982, p.4

2. See Peter Proudfoot, *The Secret Plan of Canberra*, University of NSW Press, 1994; Sarah Rossbach, *Feng Shui*, Rider 1984; Andrea Dixon, 'Home builders turn to ancient Chinese beliefs', *Sydney Morning Herald*, May 11, 1994, p.41

Appendix 2

1. Hugo Grotius, *The Law of War and Peace*, p.242

2. *Psychology Today*, July/August, 1992, p.29

3. *Truth in Religion*, Collier Books, 1990, pp.109–110

4. Excerpt from Francis Beckwith, 'Illusion of Technique', an unpublished poem dated 1982

5. See Robert Banks, *All The Business of Life*, Albatross, 1987

6. Romans 8: 22

7. Psalm 19

8. As quoted in Leo Buscaglia, *Personhood*, p.118.

9. *What is the New Age Saying to the Church?*, Marshall Pickering, 1991, p.237

10. James Sire, *Scripture Twisting*, InterVarsity Press, 1980, p.18